hot licks

hot licks

Great Recipes for Making and Cooking with Hot Sauces

Jennifer Trainer Thompson

Illustrations by Mercedes McDonald

CHRONICLE BOOKS

San Francisco

Book and cover design: Brenda Rae Eno
Calligraphy: Georgia Deaver
Composition: TBH/Typecast, Inc.

Library of Congress Cataloging-in-Publication Data

Trainer Thompson, Jennifer.
    Hot licks : great recipes for making and cooking with hot sauces /
by Jennifer Trainer Thompson; illustrations by Mercedes McDonald.
        p.   cm.
    Includes bibliographical references and index.
    ISBN 8-8118-0575-1
    1. Cookery (Hot pepper sauces) 2. Hot pepper sauces. I. Title.
TX819.H66T73   1994
641.6'384—dc20   93-6087
                                                                 CIP

Printed in Hong Kong.

Distributed in Canada by Raincoast Books,
112 East Third Ave., Vancouver, B.C. V5T 1C8

10 9 8 7 6 5 4 3 2 1

Chronicle Books
275 Fifth Street
San Francisco, CA 94103

This book is dedicated to Joseph,
my partner and pilot on the trail of flame
and elsewhere

Acknowledgments

Many people gave generously of their time and talent to make this book a reality—and fun along the way. They include Johanne Killeen and George Germon, Ted Klamm, Mark Militello, Mark Kiffin and Mark Miller, Jeff Oakley, Chris Schlesinger, and Jaimie Shannon, who demonstrate their hot stuff nightly at some of the nation's best restaurants and were generous enough to share their secrets. Also Darra Goldstein, Mary Goodbody, Mary Jane Thompson, and Elizabeth Wheeler, who were inspired with their own hot licks; Robin Brickman, Chris Duble, Nancy Duble, Coyne Edmison, Stuart Krichevsky, Sarah Purcell, Richard and Carolyn Thompson, and Ellie and Potter Trainer, who exhibited great taste; and Bob West, who was kind enough to share his wine sensibilities with me.

Others, too, kept me going on the hot licks trail—Parker Hydon, Nancy Vaughan and USAir, La Posada de Albuquerque, the Four Seasons in Austin, the Windsor Court Hotel, Nottoway Plantation, and The Sugar Mill. Thanks, too, to Leslie Jonath and Bill LeBlond at Chronicle, who didn't mind that I sent them Death Wish a week before my deadline.

Finally, this book would not have been possible without the hundreds of people in the food business who talked with me about hot sauce and encouraged this effort, especially Strat Cyrus, Malcolm Dykes, Wendy and Tim Eidson, the kind folks at Frieda's, Terry Hanes, Ken Hopkins and Grady Brown, Jose Marmolejo, Doug McDougall, and Paul McIlhenny. Thanks, too, to Jim and Diana Starke, who probably don't realize that our conversations on their porch in Vieques, smelling the herbs and tasting the heat, first led me down the hot sauce trail.

CONTENTS

INTRODUCTION

I was introduced to hot pepper sauces 14 years ago, on a sailboat delivery from West Palm Beach to the British Virgin Islands. Plagued with motor trouble and then a broken mast stay, my companions and I were forced to land on a small, outer island in the Bahamian chain.

Tropical, remote, and with no discernable tourism industry, San Salvador had one phone (which was out of order at the time) and several dirt-floor bars that served food. Heading for the nearest one, we found a king-sized jukebox with dozens of reggae songs—and every Rolling Stones record known to man. We were in heaven.

Ordering a round of rum punches and fritters, the crew settled in for a lazy afternoon. When the fritters arrived with no ketchup, I picked up the only table condiment—a recycled rum bottle with a pretty, pale-yellow sauce flecked with orange—and liberally doused my fritters. Having been at sea for a week, I wolfed down the first few fritters, and within moments I was socked with an intense pain that threatened to tear off the roof of my mouth. My companions—who had definitely sailed these waters before—howled with laughter as tears streamed down my cheeks and I discovered Caribbean hot sauces and their main ingredient: the incendiary Scotch bonnet pepper.

Minutes later, however, I found myself going back for more of this fiery potion. Once I had gotten past the pain, the sauce had actually tasted rather good. Very gingerly, then a bit more bravely, I dabbed the thickish liquid on my food. My mouth again experienced an incredible rush of heat, but also fruity flavors, and, in a few moments, I felt a distinct—almost floating—sense of well-being. It wasn't until years later that I learned that chiles cause the brain to release endorphins, a natural pain killer that stimulates the body and triggers a sense of euphoria.

Soon I was shaking hot sauce on almost everything, from soups and stews to shishkebabs and rice. But when I flew back to the States and settled into a publishing job in New York, I forgot about the "San Salvador Special" once the bottle I'd tucked into my duffel bag was gone. It wasn't until several years later, when my husband and I started spending time on Vieques, a small island between Puerto Rico and St. Thomas, that I noticed the familiar bottle at restaurant tables. Like other Caribbean islands, Vieques has its own, uniquely flavored hot sauces, which reflect the individual predilections of their makers as much as the colonizing influences that have shaped the culinary heritage of the islands in the West Indies.

Delighted by our find, we brought home cases of the sauce as gifts for friends. We were greeted with blank stares, however. "Looks great—but what do we do with it?" they asked. For many, exposure to hot sauce had been limited to McIlhenny's Tabasco brand, which in many New England households ranked bar status next to vodka, with a few drops used judiciously in Bloody Marys.

By now my husband and I were deep into hot sauce, and shared our favorite recipes with friends. On trips to the Southwest, Louisiana, and the Caribbean, we collected and compared brands—not only the traditional Louisiana varieties but also obscure Caribbean and regional concoctions whose names—Voodoo Jerk Slather, Jamaica Hell Fire, Bessie's Soul Sauce, and Hot Sauce From Hell—bespeak the obsession and good humor that hot sauce induces.

In my travels, I soon discovered that hot sauces have a passionate— some would say cult— following. In Albuquerque, I attended a Fiery Foods Show where people sported "chilehead" T-shirts and a man from Connecticut arrived with a "Heat Seeking Missile" sign affixed to his car. At a dinner in New York, I met an artist who waxed rhapsodic about driving hundreds of miles out of his way to find a particular hot sauce in Scotland. In Texas, I found a hot-sauce tasting bar with over 265 blistering samples. Back home, my Federal Express carrier—a hot-sauce man himself—told of a restaurant in upstate New York where the chef dares guests to sample his

Armageddon hot sauce, then rewards survivors by listing their names on his Wall of Flame.

Though interest in hot sauces is enjoying a dramatic surge in the United States and Europe, they've been used since prehistoric times. Arawak Indians in the Caribbean used pepper juices for seasoning and preserving food in pre-Columbian times, and a staple of the Mexican diet for centuries has been the basic red chile sauce. Christopher Columbus as well as other Spanish and Portuguese explorers in the late 1400s were responsible for introducing the chile plant to the Old World, and its spread along the trade routes to West Africa, India, and the Far East led to pungent sauces that include the West African Pili Pili and Nam Prik in Thailand. Records show that British slave ships in the 1780s served a "slabber sauce" of palm oil, water, flour, and peppers to African slaves, and there are still strong West and Central African influences in Creole and Caribbean dishes.

In the United States as early as 1807, a New Hampshire farmer and herbalist reported finding bottled cayenne pepper sauce in Newburyport, Massachusetts. An 1853 advertisement in a New Orleans newspaper treated the arrival of pepper sauce at a local druggist with the enthusiasm reserved today for fresh morels. Today, Louisiana-style hot sauces are found on most tables throughout the South to flavor "everything except dessert," as one Southerner put it. In other parts of the country—Southern California, Georgia, Miami, Chicago, New York, and the Southwest—strong ethnic influences have increased interest in hot foods in general, and in hot sauces in particular.

The Japanese and the Germans are two of the largest foreign consumers of hot sauce, which can be traced back to post-war occupation when GIs flavored hamburgers and fries with the bottled heat and it caught on with the locals, as well as the McIlhenny Company's international marketing efforts in the 1950s. In the Middle East, consumption by the

Arabs—who have been known to douse a single serving of beans with a 3-ounce bottle—dates back to the Louisiana and Texas boys who worked desert oil fields and ordered in hot sauce by the gallons.

Heat, of course, is the source of hot sauce's magic, but once you get beyond the heat, you soon discover an aromatic world rich in flavors, strongly influenced by the choice of peppers and the particular blend of fruit and spices that makes each sauce unique. Indeed, though I have come to love the searing bite of a good hot sauce, the more subtle strength of this remarkably versatile condiment lies in the range of flavors that are manifested under, over, and after the heat. The timing of the heat, and its location in your mouth, are also integral components of the hot sauce experience. As you become familiar with different hot sauces, you will be able to play them like a ten-piece jazz band, syncopating heat and flavor in time and space.

You don't have to be a macho chilehead to fall in love with hot sauces, nor do you have to blister your mouth to enjoy them at the table and in cooking. You'll find that they're very easy to make, and I urge you to incorporate them—as well as the many fine bottled hot sauces on the market—into myriad dishes, to make the flavors sing.

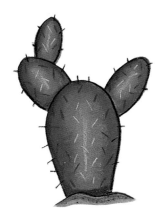

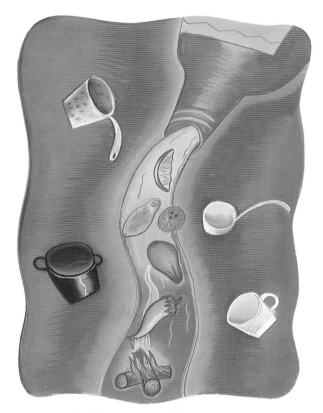

A PEPPER PRIMER

The heart of hot sauce is the chile pepper, which is thought to have originated at least 8,000 years ago in the Amazon jungle of present-day Bolivia, where birds and people spread them through South and Central America, the Caribbean, and the Southwestern region of North America. Landing in the Caribbean in 1492, Columbus mistook chiles for black peppercorns and dubbed them "peppers," thus beginning a nomenclature confusion that persists to this day. To avoid further confusion: bell peppers are sweet, chiles or chile peppers are the fiery pods, chili refers to the Texas stew, and Chile refers to the country.

If you haven't cooked much with chiles, here are a few helpful hints:

PICKING FRESH PEPPERS: Fresh chiles should have a tight, glossy flesh, with no cuts or bruises. If your grocer's selection of fresh chiles is poor, you might ask the produce manager to special order them; mine has procured fresh habañeros for me in the dead of winter. They will keep for several weeks if refrigerated in a paper bag.

DRIED PEPPERS: If fresh chiles aren't available, dried chiles can easily be substituted. To reconstitute, soak them in a pot of hot (not boiling) water until soft (about 20 minutes), keeping them submerged while soaking with a small lid. When buying dried chiles, look for unbroken skins that aren't brittle. The drying process intensifies the flavors wonderfully, so select aromatic ones. Store chiles in an airtight container in a cool place.

ROASTING PEPPERS: This easy process imparts much flavor and can be done with a broiler or stovetop. Simply put fresh chiles under the broiler (or hold over a gas flame) and rotate until they are blackened and blistered all over. Transfer the chiles to a bowl and cover with a cloth for 10 minutes (to steam and make peeling easier). When cooled, peel away the burned skin, taking care not to wash the chiles, which will rob them of the smoky flavor. Cut out the stem, seeds, and ribs. If you aren't using the chiles immediately, put them in a container, cover with olive oil, and refrigerate for up to 2 weeks. To roast dried chiles, preheat oven to 250 degrees and slit each chile (as you would a baked potato). Roast chiles in the oven just until you smell them, about 3 minutes.

HANDLING PEPPERS: Be mindful that the heat of chiles is concentrated in the seeds and white interior ribs. Don't touch your eyes or face after you've handled chiles, and wash your hands with soap and warm water after handling. If you have sensitive skin, you might wear rubber globes when working with the hotter chiles. Habañeros especially will leave a tingling numbness in your finger tips after working with them bare-handed.

CONTROLLING THE HEAT: To a degree, you can regulate the heat of a dish by removing some (or all) of the seeds and ribs from the pod. Soaking whole, fresh chiles in cold, salted water for an hour or so before cooking also moderates the heat. (Also, with the heat concentrated inside the chile, you can carve a small sliver from the outer flesh and safely taste the flavor of different varieties.)

If you cook much with New Mexico red chiles, you might order a ristra—those long strings of chiles hung on balconies throughout the Southwest after the fall harvest. While New Mexicans order twice the height of each family member to keep them in chiles year round, probably a 3-foot ristra will do. They won't last in humid climates (where mold can set in), but in drier climates they should keep up to a year. If you hang a ristra in a sunny spot, it may lose color (also a sign that it's losing flavor). Before cooking, hold the pod to the light and inspect for dark blots, which indicate mold. Dried pods can be chopped for cooking, or easily reconstituted for making sauces.

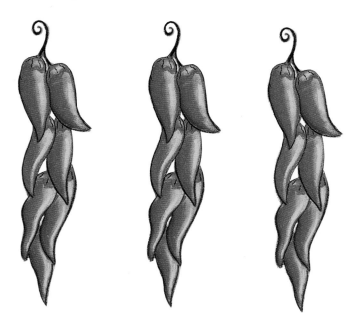

Cooking with chiles intensifies the flavors of food, but there is an added advantage: chiles are incredibly good for you. Studies have shown that peppers aid digestion and circulation, and they've been known to reduce the risk of heart disease. They're also a great source of potassium, and are rich in vitamins A, B, C, E, and P, iron, magnesium, riboflavin, niacin, and thiamin. Green chiles, for example, have twice the vitamin C found in oranges (which is why sixteenth-century Spanish sailors took chiles on voyages to prevent scurvy), and red chiles are better than carrots for vitamin A, which is essential in protecting the skin and strengthening eyesight.

Like acupuncture, jogging, and sex, chiles can also induce a glowing sense of well-being. The source of this physiological reaction is capsaicin (pronounced cap-SAY-i-sin), a chemical produced at the stem-end of the chile's placenta. As capsaicin travels from the pepper's inner sanctum to your own, it triggers a series of chemical events: first, the chemical excites the pain-detecting nerves in your mouth, nose, and throat. Thus awakened, they dispatch a pain messenger to the brain. The brain, in turn, releases natural pain killers called endorphins, which block the burning attack and trigger a "rush" of pleasurable relief. (It's not surprising that chile peppers come from the psychotropic plant family, which also includes poppies and psilocybin mushrooms.) Andrew Weil, a physician who has studied psychotropic plants, calls the experience "mouth surfing," where people "glide along on the strong stimulation, experiencing it as something between pleasure and pain that enforces concentration and brings on a high state of consciousness."

If you're not familiar with chiles, fear not—you have a wonderful adventure awaiting you. Using the recipes that follow, you can easily make great hot sauces with just a few varieties.

hot licks

Hot sauce is a dramatic culinary gesture. Soulful, jazzy, and slightly addictive, it will loosen your cooking style and add punch and flavor to a wide range of foods. When I'm cooking, hot sauce sometimes takes a lead role, and at other times it's used so subtly that it's difficult to discern the source of the wonderfully fruity flavors brought to a dish. Indeed, hot sauces are great cross-dressers—fashioning themselves as condiments, salad dressings, pizza toppings, sandwich spreads, barbecue sauces and marinades, or even taken straight as dips.

While almost all hot sauces feature chiles and a liquid base of vinegar or water, they can differ vastly and include a wide array of ingredients, from tropical fruits and vegetables to Indian curries and Southwestern spices. Sometimes hot sauces are cooked, although not always—the simplest ones consist of whole chiles steeped in vinegar, and while most will pour from a narrow-necked bottle, some are slightly chunky and others are thicker than ketchup.

Given this range, how do hot sauces differ from salsas or picante sauces? Definitions become vague as salsas (which means "sauces" in Spanish) get thinner and hot sauces get thicker. In general, however, salsas are uncooked condiments that feature chopped tomatoes or fruits (along with chiles and other ingredients). Picante sauces are slightly smoother blends that still feature tomatoes as a main ingredient. Hot sauces—unlike other sauces—contain chiles as the primary ingredient, which more often than not are pureed with other ingredients into a smooth, pourable sauce.

Chiles provide the piquancy of hot sauce, and are also essential for texture, color, and flavor. The habañero pepper, for example, has a scorching heat (up to 60 times hotter than the jalapeño) that quickly recedes, leaving a fresh fruity flavor. Chipotles have a subtle, lingering heat and a smoky flavor with woody undertones. (For information on specific chiles, see page 116.)

While selecting chiles is the first step in creating great hot sauce, balancing their taste and heat with other flavors is equally important. Good hot sauces often have complementary flavors—be it sweet-hot, smoky-sharp, earthy-acid—that dance around and flourish with the heat in marvelously subtle ways. In making a sauce, I first consider the sweet component (and it needn't be obviously sweet), which can be provided either by the chiles themselves (dried anchos, pasillas, and pullas all have fruity undertones) or by other ingredients such as tropical fruits (papayas and mangoes, for example). Sweeteners such as dark rum, sugar, honey, or molasses are also often used, as are spices ranging from ginger to allspice. (Sweet ingredients also counter and delay the heat of chiles, which is why Caribbean hot sauces with papaya and enough habañeros to send you to the moon are not unbearably hot.)

Next, I consider a sauce's acidity, which gives it verve and lift and helps prolong shelf-life. The traditional source is vinegar, which remains the main ingredient in Louisiana hot sauces. Other sources of acidity include limes, lemons, and oranges, as well as tomatoes and tomatillos.

To round out a sauce and give it depth and complexity, the pepper base is often augmented by herbs and spices, which can range from Indian sauces that incorporate a dozen spices, to simple island brews that include a sprig of fresh thyme. Mustard is sometimes used, as are nutmeg and oregano. Vegetables too, play a role in adding body and flavor, with carrots appearing often in Caribbean-style sauces.

With all the sauces, don't feel constrained by the recipes. Hot sauces flourish under an experimental hand, and do not require the timing and technique of, say, French cream sauces. Though some distinctive chiles, like the chipotle or habañero, make substitutions difficult, most chiles can be interchanged with fascinating and almost always successful results.

Although as geographic boundaries and culinary trends shift it becomes difficult to categorize many hot sauces, a road map is in order. In this chapter, hot sauces are grouped by either origin (Louisiana, the

Caribbean), flavor (Smoky Sauces), or type (Piques and Sherries). While you'll undoubtedly enjoy making your own hot sauces, you may also want to use commercial brands in your cooking, and so at the end of each grouping I've included a listing of similar bottled brands. (With over a thousand hot sauces on the market, this is a very small sampling indeed, and I encourage you to experiment with little-known brands you might discover in your travels.) Bottled hot sauces can also be used instead of homemade hot sauces in Part II (Eat the Heat).

In closing, I must say that, besides the flavor and flame of hot sauces, I also love the inventive names. Considering that chiles are called everything from Mademoiselle Jacques's Behind (habañeros in Guadaloupe) to Monkey's Little Dick (pequins in Peru), it's not surprising that a Mexican hot sauce named Pico de Gallo translates into "Bite of the Rooster," that Xnipec is Mayan for "Dog's Breath," and that in Martinique the elegant-sounding Sauce Chien means "Dog Sauce" to the locals. Hot sauce makers are carrying on the tradition—mail-order sources on page 123 will lead you to Inner Beauty, Hellfire & Damnation, or Capital Punishment ("legal in all fifty states"). Look further to call 911, Mrs. Dog, or the Gecko. No doubt, the true hot sauce believer will ask for Religious Experience, and probably request Last Rights. Failing that, then at least Jump Up and Kiss Me.

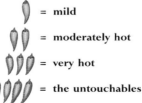

Hot sauce heat levels are denoted by a chile pepper code:

= mild

= moderately hot

= very hot

= the untouchables

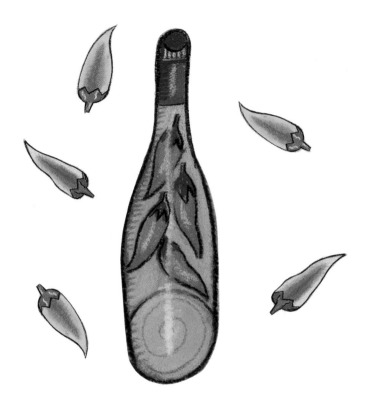

PIQUES AND SHERRIES

Made by steeping whole chiles in vinegar, unmarked piques are often found at native restaurants in the Caribbean, with fancier labeled versions available at shops in the United States. With their high vinegar content, piques will keep for up to a year unrefrigerated, except those containing fruit juice, which should be refrigerated after opening. Pepper sherry (or rum) sauces are made by steeping chiles in various spirits.

PIQUE

This hot sauce makes a beautiful holiday gift. Look for wide-mouthed bottles (in the Caribbean, I've seen piques in recycled juice, barbecue sauce, and rum bottles), which will make your pepper-packing easy. You can use any fresh or dried chiles—your choice should be driven by the bottle size, as well as the flavor, color, and heat of the chiles. I like the beautiful brick-colored New Mexico reds for large bottles, but serranos fit nicely into small bottles and pack many times the heat. Piques are especially good on green vegetables, or with rice and beans or stews.

        2 (10-ounce) bottles, sterilized
   2 to 4 dried New Mexico red chiles (or other long red chiles, such as
                cayenne)
        2 fresh habañero chiles
   2 to 4 fresh Thai chiles (or serranos or jalapeños)
   2 to 4 medium garlic cloves, peeled
        2 cups distilled or white wine vinegar (see Note)
        2 sprigs fresh rosemary or thyme

To roast the dried chiles, preheat the oven to 250 degrees, and dry-roast them just until you smell them, about 3 minutes. (Overcooking may turn the chiles bitter, and undercooking will not impart the desirable smoky flavor.) Reconstitute them by submerging them in a pot of hot water and soaking them until soft, about 20 minutes.

Clean and soften the fresh peppers and garlic in a pot of boiling water for 3 minutes. Heat the vinegar in a nonreactive saucepan to just below the boiling point. Divide the peppers and garlic between the two bottles, and fill with vinegar. Add a sprig of fresh rosemary or thyme to each, and seal. Let bottles sit in a dark place for 2 weeks, turning occasionally.

Makes 2 bottles.

Note: While white wine vinegar is often preferred for its subtle, light flavor, the harsher white distilled vinegar is also sometimes used, especially in the Caribbean, where piques with a high vegetable content benefit from the added preservative strength of distilled vinegar. Distilled vinegar, traditionally used in pickling, is also much cheaper.

> A charter pilot from Barbados told me that, when he was growing up, his kitchen table always had on it a bottle of pique, which his mother made with peppers that grew outside the back door. As the bottle neared empty, she'd add more vinegar to the peppers (and a little white rum to preserve the color and clarity), along with a pinch of salt and turmeric.

SHERRY PEPPER SAUCE

Nineteenth-century Royal sailors stationed in Bermuda fortified their sherry with hot peppers for a piquant "seasoning," an island tradition that continues to this day. Try the delightfully simple sauce below or the fancier version available from Yeaton Duval Outerbridge, an eighth-generation Bermudian whose family has been steeping bud peppers with herbs and spices in casks of sherry for over 30 years. Use a few drops of this sauce or Outerbridge's Original to enhance fish chowder, martinis, rummy drinks, or onion tarts.

30 chiltepin chiles
1 cup dry sherry

Pop these tiny, pearl-shaped peppers in a pretty glass container and pour in the sherry. Allow to stand for several days before using.
Makes 1 cup.

PIQUE AND SHERRY BOTTLED BRANDS

- **Andy's Ol' Timey Pepper Sauce.** All natural.
- **Isla Vieques Pique.** With recao. All natural.
- **Outerbridge's Original Sherry Peppers Sauce.** From Bermuda. All natural.
- **Busha Browne's Spicy and Hot Pepper Sherry.** From Jamaica. All natural.

LOUISIANA-STYLE SAUCES

Traditionally Louisiana hot sauces are fire-engine red, made with cayenne peppers (or, in the case of the McIlhenny Company, with tabasco peppers), vinegar, and salt. Some of the newer Louisiana-style sauces, however, are made with jalapeños and serranos (making them green or khaki-colored), and include spices, sweeteners, and preservatives. Louisiana hot sauces are always relatively thin, with the good ones more flavorful than merely a hot vinegar. They needn't be refrigerated, and should be replaced after a year since the vinegar predominates as the vinegar ages.

LOUISIANA RED

True Louisiana hot sauces are aged for 4 months to 3 years—and so I include this shortcut recipe as a novelty more than anything else.

- 2 *pounds finely chopped cayenne or tabasco chiles*
- 3 *cups distilled white vinegar*
- 2 *teaspoons salt*

In a medium, nonreactive saucepan, combine the chiles and vinegar and heat to just below boiling. Add the salt and simmer for 5 minutes. Puree the mixture in a blender. Pour into a container and allow to sit for at least 3 weeks. Pour through strainer into sterilized bottle.

Lord Kitchener took it with him in 1896 on his relief expedition to Khartoum. It was standard fare in the mess kits of World War I doughboys. Astronauts took it into space aboard the Skylab space station. On a remote island in south Louisiana, the McIlhenny family has been making Tabasco ever since Edmund McIlhenny returned to his plantation after the Civil War and found, amongst devastation, a few surviving tabasco plants. Experimenting with a friend's recipe, he mashed the chiles, added vinegar and salt, and aged the sauce in white oak barrels. In 1868, he sent 350 samples in used cologne bottles to likely wholesalers; today over 75 million bottles of the piquant sauce are sold yearly in over 100 countries. The King of Tonga carries a bottle wherever he goes, and the McIlhennys even know of a man who orders by the gallon—every three months.

Legend has it that Baton Rouge ("red stick" in French) was named after a pepper-picking process whereby Louisiana workers would carry into the fields a stick painted the red of a perfectly ripe pepper.

LOUISIANA-STYLE BOTTLED BRANDS

- **Andre's Rouge.** With jalapeños, honey, and Worcestershire sauce.
- **Arizona Gunslinger.** Louisiana-style from Arizona, with jalapeños.
- **Bat's Brew.** With habañeros and jalapeños.
- **Chef Hans' Louisiana Hot Pepper Sauce.** With onions and spices.
- **Crystal Pure Hot Sauce.** Smooth and dark red.
- **D. L. Jardine's Texas Champagne.** Texas, of course, has its own "Louisiana." All natural.
- **Dos Gringos.** With jalapeños, from Colorado. All natural.
- **Dr. J's Habañero Chile Elixir.** Dated by vintage year.
- **Firey Louisiana Hot Sauce.** Crisp, vinegary flavor.
- **Frank's Original RedHot.** All natural.
- **Hot Lava.** Slightly volcanic, and spicy.
- **Louisiana Original Hot Sauce.** The real thing. All natural.
- **Ortega Hot Sauce.** All natural.
- **Sho Nuff New Orleans Hot Stuff.** Medium-thick and tangy.
- **Tabasco.** Razor sharp. All natural.
- **Tennessee Sunshine.** Flavorful and all natural.
- **Vampfire.** Blood red and garlic free, with habañeros.

CARIBBEAN-STYLE SAUCES

I define "Caribbean" as the often-scorching sauces from the Caribbean lit-toral that feature habañeros, tropical fruits or vegetables, and herbs or spices. Those with fruit or vegetables should be refrigerated after opening.

SPICY ISLAND HOT SAUCE

Papayas give Caribbean hot sauces body and a lush, tropical flavor, while at the same time turning them into natural meat tenderizers. Although green unripe papayas have more tenderizing properties (skin one and you'll see the white milky liquid), the ripe ones contribute such a tropical flavor that some hot sauce makers include both unripe and ripe papayas in their sauces.

Enlivened with nutmeg, cardamom, cinnamon, and other spices, this sauce makes a good crudité dip. I also incorporate it into entrees, where the strong, spicy flavors suffuse the main course with an exotic, aromatic appeal—not unlike a light curry.

1 ripe papaya, peeled, seeded, and coarsely chopped
1 medium yellow onion, coarsely chopped
2 medium garlic cloves, minced
4 Scotch bonnet or habañero peppers, stemmed and seeded
  1-inch length fresh ginger, peeled and coarsely chopped
⅓ cup dark rum
⅓ cup fresh lime juice
½ teaspoon salt
2½ teaspoons honey
⅛ teaspoon cardamom
⅛ teaspoon anise
⅛ teaspoon cloves
⅛ teaspoon turmeric
  Pinch nutmeg
  Pinch cinnamon
  Freshly ground black pepper to taste

Combine all ingredients in blender and puree just until smooth, or about 1 minute (taking care not to overblend and aerate). Pour into a saucepan and bring to a boil, then simmer gently, uncovered, for 10 minutes. Remove from heat and allow to cool before bottling. Refrigerated, the sauce will keep approximately 6 weeks.

Makes 2 cups.

WEST INDIAN PEPPER SAUCE

In the West Indies, tropical fruits abound—trees are dense with mangoes, papayas, and coconuts—and kitchen gardens have many peppers, which are blended into scorching sauces. Typically Caribbean, this sauce is versatile as an all-around hot condiment. The color of the peppers will affect the tones of the sauce—I prefer three yellow and one orange habañero, which yields a lemon-yellow sauce with flecks of orange.

1   ripe mango or papaya
1   medium yellow onion, coarsely chopped
1   medium garlic clove
5   Scotch bonnet or habañero chiles, stemmed (but not seeded)
    1-inch piece ginger root, coarsely chopped
½   teaspoon turmeric
1   tablespoon dry mustard
    Pinch of cumin
    Pinch of coriander
½   tablespoon honey
½   cup cider vinegar
½   cup water
1   teaspoon salt

In a blender, puree the mango, onion, garlic, chiles, ginger root, turmeric, mustard, cumin, coriander, and honey. Transfer mixture to a bowl.

In a nonreactive saucepan, bring the vinegar, water, and salt to a boil. Pour over mango mixture and stir well. Allow to cool before bottling. Refrigerated, the sauce will keep approximately 6 weeks.

Makes 2 cups.

MANGO SCOTCH BONNET BARBECUE SAUCE

In this barely hot yet delicious sauce, Mark Militello of Mark's Place in North Miami combines the slightly sweet tomato base of traditional barbecue sauces with the tropical flavor of the Scotch bonnet pepper and a complex palette of spices. One of the more complicated sauces presented here, it is typical of the sophisticated dishes coming from new American cooking. Spicy-sweet, it's especially well suited for fish steaks, or as a dipping sauce for grilled vegetables.

> 1 green bell pepper, halved and cored
> 1 red bell pepper, halved and cored
> 2 fresh tomatoes, peeled, seeded, and halved
> 1½ ripe mangoes
> ½ Spanish onion
> 2 garlic cloves
> 1 Scotch bonnet or habañero chile, stemmed
> 6 tablespoons cider vinegar
> ¼ pound brown sugar
> ⅛ cup molasses
> ⅛ cup Dijon mustard
> ⅛ cup tamarind pulp
> 1 tablespoon cinnamon
> ½ tablespoon cumin
> ½ tablespoon thyme leaf
> ½ tablespoon marjoram
> Salt and freshly ground black pepper to taste
> ½ cup water

Smoke the peppers and tomatoes for 30 minutes in a home smoker fueled with oak chips (see Note).

Peel the mangoes and cut the flesh off the seeds. Chop the onion and mince the garlic. Cut the chile in half.

Combine all the ingredients in a large non-reactive saucepan. Simmer gently for 1 hour. Puree the sauce in a blender and pour it through a medium mesh strainer. Correct the seasoning, adding salt and pepper to taste.

Makes 4½ cups

Note: You can also "cool smoke" the bell peppers and tomatoes on a charcoal (or gas) grill by firing up the coals on half the grill, adding oak chips after the coals have reduced to low embers (or the gas grill is reduced to its lowest setting), and placing the vegetables on the cool side of the grill, covered, for 10 minutes. The vegetables should sweat slightly but not cook.

"Flavor before fire, mon," one West Indian advised about hot sauces, and it's best illustrated by the West Indian folktale of a Creole woman who, having tasted chiles in other dishes, decided to make a soup of just Scotch bonnet peppers. When she served it to her children, they ran down to the river to cool their inflamed mouths and, drinking too much water, all drowned.

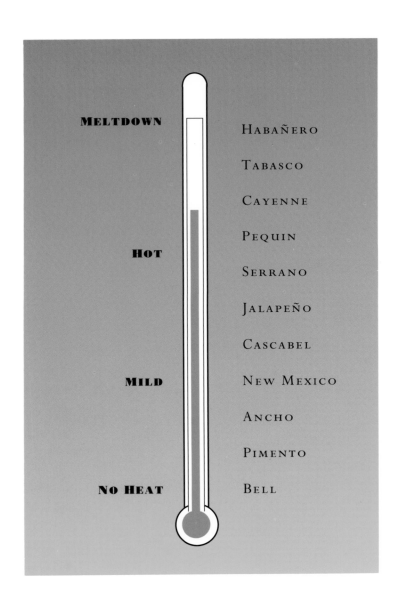

MELTDOWN

HOT

MILD

NO HEAT

HABAÑERO

TABASCO

CAYENNE

PEQUIN

SERRANO

JALAPEÑO

CASCABEL

NEW MEXICO

ANCHO

PIMENTO

BELL

PINEAPPLE CURRY HEAT WAVE

Smooth, thick, and deeply flavored with curry, this sauce has a two-fisted punch that hits immediately on your lips, then follows through with a lingering heat that lofts flavor throughout your mouth, nose, and sinuses. The pineapple makes an unusual base, and its high acid content lends a decided tropical note to the heat. This is a great all-purpose sauce. I use it straight as a table condiment and find myself reaching for it often as I cook.

12 Scotch bonnet or habañero chiles, preferably yellow or red, stemmed (but not seeded)
1 large yellow onion, chopped (about 2 cups)
1 cup fresh pineapple, diced in 1-inch cubes
4 tablespoons 100% pure pineapple juice
3 teaspoons turmeric
2 teaspoons ground dry mustard
1 teaspoon ground fenugreek
1 teaspoon ground coriander seed
1 teaspoon ground celery seed
2 teaspoons mace flakes (or 1 teaspoon ground mace)
3 teaspoons ground cumin seed
1 teaspoon ground cayenne
2 teaspoons pure, ground red chile powder
16 turns fresh black pepper
1-inch piece ginger root, minced
¼ teaspoon cornstarch
4 tablespoons cider vinegar
2 teaspoons honey

Place the chiles, onion, pineapple juice, and spices in a blender, and puree until very smooth. In a nonreactive saucepan over low heat, dissolve the cornstarch in the vinegar, add the puree and honey, and simmer slowly for 10 minutes. Cool and pour into sterilized jar. Refrigerated, the sauce will keep up to 8 weeks.

Makes 2½ cups.

F-16 AFTERBURNER

This recipe has the basic ingredients of a Caribbean hot sauce, though the Scotch bonnet peppers appear in extremis for those who care about flavor but can't get enough heat. The recipe is not named after the Navy fighter plane that starred in Desert Storm, but after the sixteen chiles that create a heat storm of their own in this sauce. In other words, this is a sauce for the chileheads whose predictable reaction to all hot sauce is, "oh, it wasn't that hot," because the F-16 takes no prisoners.

Though many Caribbean sauces feature one chile type, I also used an ancho and a fresh red chile; I like the fuller tones of the ancho, and the red chile adds a lingering heat to the hit-and-run Scotch bonnet. Perhaps just as important, the red chile contributes brilliant crimson flecks to an otherwise golden sauce, which I like to think of as little warning flags signaling the red-hot heat to come.

½ dried ancho chile
1 fresh red Dutch, Thai, or jalapeño chile
16 fresh Scotch bonnet or habañero chiles, preferably orange or golden yellow
1 cup coarsely chopped yellow onion
4 medium garlic cloves
1 tablespoon fresh lemon juice
1 tablespoon amber or light rum
1 cup distilled white vinegar
½ teaspoon dried oregano

Submerge the ancho in a pot of hot water and soak until soft, about 20 minutes. Chop ancho finely and reserve. Roast and peel the Dutch chile, as indicated on page 6. Stem, seed, and finely chop the chile.

Stem and seed the Scotch bonnets, leaving the inner membranes (and, if desired, a few seeds). Combine Scotch bonnets with onion and garlic in a food processor and process until very finely chopped. Combine lemon juice, rum, and vinegar in a nonreactive pan and bring to a boil. Pour liquid into processor, add the oregano and Dutch chile, and process lightly. Add the ancho teaspoon by teaspoon, processing briefly in between, pulsing only enough to obtain a smooth, yellow-orange sauce, highlighted by red flecks. (Overprocessing or adding too much ancho will result in a redder sauce, which is also quite beautiful.) Refrigerated, this sauce will keep 6 weeks.

Makes 2 cups.

CARIBBEAN-STYLE BOTTLED BRANDS

- ♦♦♦ **Busha Browne's Pukka Sauce.** From a nineteenth-century family recipe.

- ♦♦♦ **D. L. Jardine's Blazin' Saddle.** Habañeros, lime, onions, and carrots. All natural.

- ♦♦ **Dat'l Do-It Devil Drops.** Mango, passion fruit, and carrots. All natural.

- ♦♦♦ **Evadney's Jamaican Hot Sauce.** Thick and flavorful, with a spicy tomato base. All natural.

- ♦ **Grand Anse Moko Jumbie.** With mango, cinnamon, ginger, and strong cloves. All natural.

- ♦♦♦ **Hellfire & Damnation.** With habañeros, carrots, onions, and garlic. All natural.

- ♦♦♦♦ **Inner Beauty Real Hot Sauce.** With curry and pineapple. All natural.

- ♦♦♦♦ **Isla Vieques Caribe Fire.** Papaya-based habañero sauce. Also **Mountain Herb Hot Sauce (♦♦♦)** and **Salsa Picante (♦♦♦).** All natural.

- ♦♦♦ **Island Treasure Papaya Pepper Sauce.** From Jamaica, with habañeros and papaya.

- ♦♦♦ **Jab-Jab.** From Trinidad, with habañeros, papaya, and lime.

- ♦♦♦ **Jamaica Hell Fire Doc's Special.** Tropical peppers and allspice.

- ♦♦♦ **Jump Up and Kiss Me.** Habañeros in a fruit base. All natural.

- ♦♦♦♦ **Matouk's.** From Trinidad, in ketchup-sized bottles.

Melinda's. With carrots and habañeros. All natural.

Mrs. Dog's. Habañeros, Portugal peppers, and allspice.

Papaya Pepper Tropic Hot Sauce. With papaya and other ingredients from the rain forest.

Pickapeppa Hot Sauce. A sweet, Jamaican sauce with mangoes, raisins, and tamarind. All natural.

Rebel Fire No. 3. Scotch bonnets, mango, and curry.

Salu's Scotch Bonnet Pepper Sauce. A thick Jamaican sauce with mustard.

Sontava Hot Sauce. Habañeros, carrots, lime, and garlic. All natural.

Spitfire Hot Pepper Sauce. From Barbados, with horseradish and mustard. All natural.

Sunny Caribbee Hot Sauce. From Tortola.

Trinidad Habañero Pepper Sauce. With Trinidad herbs and spices.

Uncle Billy's Voo Doo Jerk Slather. With honey, Spanish onions, molasses, and tamarind.

West Indies Creole Hot Pepper Sauce. Papaya-based sauce that pours like a Louisiana red. All natural.

Yucatan Sunshine. A good, mild introduction to habañeros. All natural.

SAUCE OF THE BORDER

These sauces are often distinguished by the use of a particular chile (casabel, chipolte, pequin, or New Mexico Red), with earthy ingredients ranging from tomatoes and onions to pumpkin seeds and carrots. Most of these sauces hail from New Mexico, Texas, or Mexico.

SMOKY SALSA PICANTE

Just looking at the gnarly chipotle, you can sense its depth of flavor and mystery. Too thick-fleshed to air dry, fresh jalapeños are placed in large, underground pits, which are connected by a tunnel system to a central firebox. Here, hardwoods are stoked for days to produce the smoke that eventually transmogrifies jalapeños into the shadowy chipotle—or, if mesquite is used and the peppers are pulled from the pits a day early, the slightly more robust mora chiles.

To highlight the chipotle's smoky flavor, this salsa picante ("hot sauce" in Spanish) is not as hot as others, but it still has a kick. You can reduce its heat by removing the chile seeds and using ½ teaspoon of ground cayenne, but would that be any fun?

 6 *chipotles, or moras*
 1 *small, green, unripe papaya*
 6 *fresh, red jalapeños, stemmed (or other hot, red chiles)*
 1 *small yellow onion*
 1 *carrot*
 3 *medium garlic cloves*
 2 *sprigs fresh cilantro*
 1 *large fresh basil leaf*
 1 *cup water*
 ¾ *cup malt or cider vinegar*
 ¼ *teaspoon allspice*
 1 *teaspoon ground cayenne*
 ½ *teaspoon salt*
  Freshly ground black pepper to taste

Reconstitute the chipotles by submerging them in a pot of hot water and soaking until soft, about 20 minutes.

In a nonreactive saucepan, boil the papaya until tender, about 15 minutes. Cool, peel, remove the seeds, and cut into chunks. Combine in a blender with chiles, onion, carrot, garlic, cilantro, and basil, and pulse until finely chopped.

Add the water, vinegar, allspice, cayenne, salt, and pepper and puree until smooth, or about 1 minute. Take care not to overblend. Pour into saucepan and bring to a boil. Lower heat and simmer, uncovered, for 10 minutes. Remove from heat and allow to cool before bottling. Refrigerated, the sauce will keep up to 6 weeks.

Makes 2 cups.

CHIPOTLE RED SAUCE

This deep, reddish-brown sauce combines chipotle chiles with dried New Mexico red chiles and anchos. The cocoa—borrowed from Mexican mole sauces—doesn't sweeten the sauce; rather, it adds a mellowness that, combined with the orange juice, takes the sometimes bitter edge off the dried chiles. This sauce has great range: it is "big" enough to be used as a marinade for grilled meats and is also a fine steak sauce that's not too sweet. Not particularly searing, it is also a wonderful dipping accompaniment to grilled chicken and fish. My favorite dish for this sauce, however, is Fajitas (page 80), where the onions, peppers, steak, and warm tortillas come alive with the smoky chipotles.

5	*dried chipotle chiles (see Note)*
2	*dried New Mexico red chiles*
1	*dried ancho chile*
6	*medium garlic cloves, unpeeled*
1½	*cups water or chile water (see below)*
¾	*teaspoon salt*
6	*tablespoons cider vinegar*
1	*teaspoon unsweetened cocoa*
2	*tablespoons dark brown sugar*
¼	*teaspoon ground cumin*
1	*cup fresh orange juice*
¼	*teaspoon ground cloves*
½	*teaspoon ground cayenne*

Preheat oven to 250 degrees. Stem and slit all the dried chiles, removing half the seeds. (For a milder sauce, remove all the seeds.) Roast the chiles in the oven just until you smell them, about 3 minutes maximum. Submerge them in a pot of hot water and soak until softened, about 20 minutes.

While the chiles are soaking, turn oven up to 500 degrees. Roast the garlic on a baking sheet for 20 minutes, then peel.

Taste the chile water. If it's not bitter, use it instead of water. Combine the chiles, garlic, chile water, salt, vinegar, cocoa, sugar, cumin, orange juice, cloves, and ¼ teaspoon cayenne in blender and puree. Taste, and add an additional ¼ teaspoon cayenne if greater heat is desired. Pour into sterilized bottle and seal. Refrigerated, the sauce will keep approximately 8 weeks.

Makes 3 cups.

Note: You may substitute canned chipotles in adobo, which will make roasting and soaking unnecessary. Lift the chipotles from the sauce, but don't rinse, as the adobo adds flavor.

HOT SMOKE FINISHING SAUCE

Though this sauce can be used as a marinade or as a dressing for vegetables, I prefer it as a "finishing" sauce to brush over meats during the last minute on the grill. Its rich, smoky flavor comes from the chipotles, with the heat provided by your hot pepper of choice. The bourbon's oak tones make this finishing sauce a perfect companion to Joe's Soak Sauce (see page 38), with the maple syrup lending it a distinctive flavor that makes bottled barbecue sauces seem one-dimensional by comparison.

¼ cup olive oil

1 medium yellow onion, coarsely chopped

6 medium garlic cloves, minced

1 tablespoon brown sugar

⅓ cup maple syrup

¼ cup bourbon

1 cup cider vinegar

½ teaspoon allspice

½ teaspoon nutmeg

½ teaspoon ground thyme

½ teaspoon cinnamon

1 tablespoon ground coriander

1 tablespoon unsweetened dark cocoa powder

8 medium, dried chipotles, stemmed, or canned chipotles

1 fresh habañero chile, stemmed (or hot pepper of choice)

1 bottle (14 ounces) ketchup

1½ cups water

Salt to taste

Heat the oil in a large, heavy pot over medium heat and sauté onion and garlic until soft. Lower heat, add sugar, syrup, bourbon, vinegar, spices, and cocoa, and reduce for 5 to 10 minutes. Cut the chiles in half and add to the pot, along with the ketchup, water, and salt. Cook slowly for 1½ hours, covered, stirring occasionally and adding more water if the sauce becomes thicker than ketchup. When sauce has cooled slightly, puree in the blender. Refrigerated, the sauce will keep 2 to 3 weeks.

Makes 3½ cups.

In hot pursuit of the world's best sauce, I headed to Albuquerque for the Fiery Foods Show, an annual "meltdown" billed as the hottest show on earth. There I found chile sauces, candies, postcards . . . even lace pasties with dangling pods. (This fruit has a following; can you imagine a squash titty tassle?)

People sampled the food, sweating profusely, laughing while tears ran down their cheeks. Passing one hot-sauce lover hiccupping uncontrollably, I was reassured by his wife: "When he starts hiccupping I know he's in heaven." Baby chileheads in strollers were everywhere, being spoonfed mild salsa. At a booth for the Chile Institute of New Mexico, a serious young man from the Philippines discussed his graduate work on thousands of pepper varieties. At another, the maker of Mrs. Dog's sauce explained: "Living in Grand Rapids, I feel it's my responsibility to heat up the Midwest." While the gratuitously hot mentality prevailed in some corners, the festival overall was a lively place to discover new brands of bottled heat.

JOE'S SOAK SAUCE

Most store-bought barbecue sauces are tomato- and sugar-based, leaving a caramelized, burnt crust on meats cooked over an open fire. This sauce is vinegar-based, fired with chiles, garlic, and rosemary (not to mention bourbon, which adds a subtle sweetness). Use Joe's Soak as a marinade to soak meat for several hours before cooking it low and slow (the hallmark of real barbecue), reserving a bit of the sauce to baste the meat while grilling. Pork, ribs, chicken, and swordfish love Joe's Soak. For a real treat, during the last minute or two of cooking, top off the meat with Hot Smoke Finishing Sauce (page 36), which can also be served as a side dish to food barbecued with Joe's Soak Sauce.

>   4 dried New Mexico red chiles
>   4 dried chipotles
>   2 fresh habañero or Scotch bonnet chiles, stemmed and seeded
>   6 medium garlic cloves
>   ⅓ cup loosely packed, fresh rosemary
> 1½ teaspoon sea salt
>   ¼ cup straight bourbon
>   2 cups red wine vinegar
>   ¼ cup fresh lemon juice
>   ¼ cup coarsely chopped onions

Preheat oven to 250 degrees. Dry roast the dried chiles in the oven until you smell them, about 3 minutes. Submerge them in a pot of hot water and soak them until soft, about 20 minutes. Put all ingredients in a blender and give it hell for 3 to 4 minutes. Pour into mason jar. Joe's Soak improves with age and will last refrigerated for 6 weeks.

Makes 3 cups.

HATCH SPECIAL

This hot sauce combines the tropical fruits often found in Caribbean hot sauces with the earthy chiles of the American Southwest. The result is a rich, fruity sauce with alternating hot-sweet flavors that ride over the top of the New Mexico reds (which hail from the Hatch region of New Mexico). The serrano chiles and cayenne add a sharp accent to the New Mexico chile's rounder, woodier tones. The flecked, deep brick-red color is spectacular, and this sauce makes an excellent marinade for pork, shrimp, or turkey, especially with a dollop served on the side as garnish.

    5 dried New Mexico red chiles
    2 fresh, green serrano chiles
    2 medium garlic cloves
    ½ medium onion
    ¼ teaspoon ground cayenne
    1 ripe papaya
       Juice of 1 lime
    4 tablespoons rum
    1 tablespoon raisins
    1 ripe mango or 1 teaspoon mango chutney
    ¼ cup cilantro

Preheat oven to 250 degrees. Roast the dried chiles in the oven until you smell them, about 3 minutes. Submerge them in a pot of hot water, and soak them until soft, about 20 minutes. Reserve the chile water.

Roast the fresh serranos by holding them over a grill or burner flame with a fork, and rotating until they are blistered and blackened. Place them in a bowl under a towel, allowing the steam to loosen the skins. With your fingers, peel away the thin, outer skin. Stem and seed the chiles. (Chile-heads will want to leave some seeds for greater heat.)

In a food processor or blender, combine the dried and fresh chiles with the remaining ingredients and process until the chiles are reduced to small flecks. Add up to 3 tablespoons of chile water to thin the sauce, stopping just short of a puree. This sauce tastes best at room temperature, and will keep for 1 week refrigerated.

Makes 2½ cups.

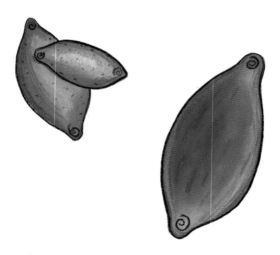

BORDER SAUCES BOTTLED BRANDS

- 🌶🌶🌶 **Bufalo Jalapeño.** A deep red Mexican sauce.

- 🌶🌶 **Cholula Hot Sauce.** From Mexico, made with the rare pequin. All natural.

- 🌶🌶 **Coyote Cocina Tangy Taco Sauce.** A pleasant tang, with New Mexico reds. Also **Smoky Chipotle Sauce,** chipotles and pasilla negros in a vinegar base (🌶🌶).

- 🌶🌶 **Desert Fire Hot Sauce.** Serranos, tomato paste, garlic and spice. Their **Ass Kickin' Hot Sauce** adds habañero for an extra boot (🌶🌶🌶).

- 🌶 **Don Alfonso Chipotles en Adobo.** Not quite a hot sauce but a good way to obtain the chipotles for one.

- 🌶🌶🌶🌶 **El Yucateco.** Small bottles and unearthly colors distinguish these intense habañero sauces.

- 🌶🌶🌶 **Hot Sauce from Hell.** The melting wax seal sets this bottle apart, as do the habañeros. All natural.

- 🌶🌶🌶 **La Gloria Chipotle Sauce.** From Mexico, with an onion and tomato base. All natural.

- 🌶 **Montezuma Chile Cascabel Sauce** contains the rare cascabel. **Devil's Tongue Hot Sauce** with pasilla negro is earthy and lightly spiced (🌶🌶). **Wild Pequin Hot Sauce** has a sharp bite (🌶🌶🌶). All natural.

- 🌶🌶 **Sante Fe Exotix Green Chile Sauce.** Chile verde with tequila gold. All natural.

- 🌶🌶🌶🌶 **Stonewall Chile Pepper Company Salsa Habañero.** Blistering hot from Texas. All natural.

SPECIALTY SAUCES
AND WORLD HEAT

This category includes sauces with unusual textures, spices, and geographic origins that fall outside the other realms.

ADZHIKA

In the Republic of Georgia, hot sauce is called adzhika (pronounced ad-ZSHEE-kah), and is found in most kitchens throughout the countryside. Unlike their Russian neighbors, Georgians love hot peppers, especially in the west, where chiles were probably brought by Ottoman Turks in the 1500s. This recipe comes from my friend Darra Goldstein, a Russian scholar and Georgian cookbook author. She reports that Georgians use adzhika many ways: as a condiment with grilled meat, as a spicy accent in stews—even as a topping over fresh melon. The dill taste is pronounced and delightful.

    10 medium garlic cloves
     2 celery stalks, including leaves, coarsely chopped
    10 red or green jalapeño chiles, coarsely chopped
     2 red bell peppers, coarsely chopped
     2 cups coarsely chopped fresh dill
    1½ cups coarsely chopped cilantro
     ½ cup red wine vinegar
     ¼ heaping teaspoon salt

In a food processor, grind the garlic slightly, using the pulse control. Add the celery, chiles, and bell peppers to the garlic and pulse again. Add the herbs and pulse to a medium-fine coarseness. Transfer the mixture to a bowl and stir in the vinegar and salt. Cover and let stand overnight.

The next day, spoon into jars. Refrigerated, the sauce will keep 3 weeks. Adzhika tastes best when allowed to sit for three days before serving.

Makes 2 cups.

PEBRE

Pebre is a popular Chilean hot sauce traditionally served as a meat or chicken accompaniment. It's also delicious atop grilled tomatoes. A lovely bright-green color, pebre has a fresh garden taste with none of the sweet undertones of many hot sauces. Although this recipe calls for only two habañeros, they are not masked by a sugar base, and their zesty heat springs forward alongside the cilantro, parsley, and garlic. Warn your guests that this is no regular steak sauce, but rather an equivalent to the hot mustard sauce served in Japanese restaurants. A judicious spoonful per serving is plenty!

1 cup olive oil
½ cup red wine vinegar
1 cup chopped yellow onion
½ cup chopped cilantro
½ cup chopped parsley
4 medium garlic cloves, minced
4 habañero chiles, stemmed
Salt and freshly ground black pepper to taste

Combine all ingredients in a blender and puree. To allow flavors to develop, let the sauce stand at room temperature for several hours before serving. Refrigerated, it will keep 1 week.

Makes 2 cups.

HARISSA

This rip-roaring North African and French hot sauce made with cayenne (called "the enraged pepper" by the French) is served with many things—stews, grilled mussels, even bread. Its thick, paste-like consistency makes it a flavorful side accompaniment to grilled meats, or it can be thinned with chile water and served over couscous.

    4 dried ancho chiles
    ⅛ cup tomato paste
    4 tablespoons olive oil
    4 teaspoons ground cayenne
    6 medium garlic cloves
    2 teaspoons cumin
    2 teaspoons coriander
    ¾ cup water or reconstituted chile water

Reconstitute the anchos by putting them in a pot of hot water and soaking until soft, about 20 minutes. While chiles are soaking, puree all the ingredients except the water in a blender or food processor.

Remove the anchos from the pot (reserving the water), stem and tear them into several pieces, and add to the blender. Taste the chile water, and if not bitter, add ¾ cup to the blender (otherwise add water). Puree until smooth. For a thinner sauce, add more chile water in small increments until you reach the desired consistency. Refrigerated, harissa will keep for several weeks.

Makes 1½ cups.

DEATH WISH

At the end of a snowmobile trail in New York's Adirondack mountains lies the Red Dog Tavern, a bar run by Ted Klamm. A former Navy Sea Dog, Ted has developed an incendiary line of hot sauces starting with Nuclear Waste and ending with his Armageddon series (I–VII). If a customer can eat ten chicken wings marinated in one of the Armageddon hot sauces, he gets his name on Red Dog's Wall of Flame. So far, only eleven have made it (and only one has survived Armageddon VII).

While not wanting to disclose his secrets, Ted shared his recipe for Death Wish, a sauce falling somewhere between Nuclear Waste and Armageddon I. Short of hopping on a snowmobile and heading to Inlet, New York, this is the closest you may get to Armageddon.

> 15 *habañero chiles, stemmed*
> 1 *bottle (7 ounces) A Taste of Thai Garlic Chili Pepper Sauce or other garlic-chile sauce*
> ¼ *cup honey ("to deaden the pain momentarily")*
> 3 *medium garlic cloves, minced*

Grind the habañeros (with seeds) in a food processor. Add other ingredients and puree.

Makes 2 cups.

DIJON DOUBLE HOT

This thick sauce features a quartet of chiles: the serranos give a lasting, lip-zipping heat while the habañeros raise the heat ante even higher, the smooth cascabels lend a mellowness, and the mild banana peppers offer an edgy vegetable flavor. This sauce is delicious in stews and salad dressings, and also as a table condiment with stir-fried meals.

8 dried cascabel chiles

32 green serrano chiles (with seeds), roasted, skinned, and stemmed

8 yellow banana chiles, roasted, skinned, and stemmed

8 fresh habañero chiles

1 cup diced carrots

1 cup diced scallions (include greens)

4 teaspoons prepared dijon mustard

4 teaspoons prepared, coarse horseradish

1 cup cider vinegar

2 teaspoons white or amber rum

2 teaspoons honey

Submerge the cascabel peppers for 20 minutes in hot water. Remove stems, slice in half, remove and discard seeds, and with a spoon scrape the tender red flesh from the outer skin. Add this pulp and remaining ingredients to a food processor and puree until very smooth. Add a few drops of water if the mixture is too thick. Refrigerated, the sauce will keep up to 6 weeks.

Makes 2 cups.

PILI PILI

This blistering West African hot sauce separates the hotheads from the rest. As common there as ketchup is here, it's used to spice up most foods—from chicken in Senegal to shrimp in Togo. Pili Pili is also popular in Portugal and Brazil (where its called Piri Piri), and is often served as a simple relish with grilled chicken, rice, and beans. Though made authentically with guinea chiles, habañeros are an acceptable substitute.

   10 *habañero chiles, stemmed*
   ½ *medium yellow onion*
   1 *medium garlic clove*
       Juice of ½ lemon
   ½ *cup olive oil*
       Pinch of oregano

Chop the chiles, onion, and garlic in a processor. Add other ingredients and blend. Refrigerated, the sauce will keep for 2 weeks.

Makes 1 cup.

Variations: In Benin, this sauce is made with a bit of fresh ginger. You could also omit the olive oil and serve Pili Pili as a thick relish with grilled meat.

FOR STORING HOT SAUCES, HANDY CONTAINERS INCLUDE

- **empty ketchup or barbecue sauce bottles**
- **5-ounce liquor bottles—the hip flasks are perfect**
- **any squirt bottles (including plastic honey bears)**

And, for your favorite hot sauces, start saving those wine bottles!

SPECIALTY BOTTLED BRANDS

Capital Punishment. Sadistically hot, this habañero sauce is a killer.

Clancy's Fancy. With honey and olive oil. All natural.

Craig's Hot Pepper Sauce. Well-spiced in a tomato base.

Hell in a Bottle. A scorcher, with applesauce.

Hot as Hell. Oriental peppers, oil, and spices. All natural.

Lingham's Chilly Sauce. This mild, spicy Malaysian sauce is a good cooking sauce. All natural.

Liquid Summer. With datil peppers, tomatoes, olive oil, and spices.

Lotta Hotta Besos de Fuego. Enough habañeros to send this "kiss of fire" off the charts.

Miz Grazi's Hot Stuff. With onions, sugar, and garlic from the banks of the Mississippi.

Pepper Creek Farms Wildfire. With horseradish. All natural.

Rebel Fire No. 2. Spicy, with African mombases, Mexican guajillos, and anchos.

Satan's Revenge. Chiles, lemon, and garlic floating in an oil base. All natural.

Starboard's Three Pepper Lemon Hot Sauce. Tabasco peppers, lemon juice, and loads of black pepper.

Tiger Sauce. Hot-sweet, all-purpose sauce.

eat the heat

Hot sauce is the bungee jumping of the culinary world. I often take mine straight up, using it liberally as a last-second shake on foods. But hot sauces can play another role as well: as a seasoning, hot sauces can be integrated into dishes so discreetly that their presence is ephemeral and wonderfully mysterious. After all, the use of black pepper in a dish doesn't always imply that a dish is "peppery." So, too, hot sauce is incorporated organically into many of the following recipes—more to spark flavor than to provoke a meltdown.

The type of hot sauce you use will make an enormous difference in a dish's outcome. The meatloaf, for example, calls for a hot sauce with habañeros, which transforms this comfort food. If you make it with a Louisiana-style hot sauce instead, you'll find a flavorful dish so mild that even kids will enjoy it.

In cooking with hot sauces, several tips will help you predict, modulate, and exploit the spicy heat of pepper sauces, and with some experimentation, you will quickly become comfortable integrating them in dishes. First, the longer a food is cooked, the more the heat dissipates. An incendiary hot sauce cooked in a casserole for 40 minutes will have far milder results than the same sauce used to marinade shrimp that is grilled briefly over live coals. Second, the heat is also absorbed and muted by starches and counteracted by acids, so dishes heavy with potatoes or tomatoes can withstand more hot sauce without becoming exceedingly hot.

Sweetness also counters the heat of hot sauces—or, more precisely, delays the sensation of heat—and therefore subdues it. Likewise, dishes with honey, maple syrup, or fruit are often given an added flavor dimension by a few shakes of hot sauce early in the cooking process. And finally, oil will keep capsaicin in contact with sensitive mouth tissues for a longer duration, thereby prolonging the heat.

In menu planning, consider the pacing of the heat—you don't want to scorch people on the hors d'oeuvres and ruin their taste buds for dinner. For large, formal dinner parties, I'll serve one side dish with a subtle zip that may be hotter than a non-chilehead might expect but that is certainly not uncomfortably hot. Caribbean-style yams or tomatoes provençal would be good choices.

For smaller, less formal dinners among friends, I might serve a spicy grilled meat or fish, though I try to use a milder seasoning on part of the dish if there are novices in the group. With grilled food, where the entire dish is marinated, I baste only a portion of it during cooking, especially since basting often produces higher heat levels than marinating. (If an entree is hot, be sure to include cooling side dishes, such as a cucumber and yogurt salad or a mixed green salad.)

The menus I enjoy most, however, are those that celebrate the flavor and heat of hot sauces in myriad ways. These are dinners for my hot food friends, where we all revel in the heat. Yet, even then, it's important to provide relief—breads, salads, cooling dips—and variety.

Invite people over for a "hot foods night" and they might surprise you. A friend of mine known for his mildness of heart and palate came to dinner, professing that he "couldn't take" hot foods. Yet, when he sampled the food—and found it flavorful and pleasing—he became the heartiest of eaters, even dabbing hot sauce on his bread. On a vacation recently to the Yucatan, he even brought back a pound of habañeros. People will fool you; many simply associate heat with temperature, not flavor, and when they experience what hot sauce brings to a dish, they become converts.

So mix yourself a Flyboy, serve up some Summer Salsa del Fuego, and enjoy those hot licks!

COCKTAILS

FLYBOY

This drink has the astringent pull that marks truly great cocktails, and also the elegance. Its inspiration resides in the Sherry Pepper Sauce. The grenadine is optional but lends the drink a peachy color that is a sight to behold in a crystal glass on a warm spring evening.

> 2 ounces gin
> Juice of ½ orange
> Dash of Sherry Pepper Sauce (page 15) or a bottled sherry sauce
>   such as Outerbridge's Original
> Dash of Angostura Bitters
> Juice of one slice of lime
> Dash of grenadine (optional)

Shake ingredients over ice until well chilled, and serve over cracked ice in a cocktail glass.

Makes 1 drink.

"I never have more than one drink before dinner, but I do like that one to be very large and very strong and very cold and very well made."
—James Bond

CLASSIC BLOODY MARY

Concocted by an American bartender at Harry's Bar in Paris in the '20s, the Bloody Mary was first spiked with Tabasco at the King Cole Bar at the St. Regis in New York in the '30s and has been served that way ever since. How powerful is a good Bloody Mary? Ernest Hemingway claimed that his Bloody Mary recipe, which he introduced to Hong Kong Society in 1941, "did more than any single factor except the Japanese army to precipitate the fall of that Crown Colony."

3 ounces vodka

4 ounces V-8 juice

Juice of 1 lemon wedge

Dash of Worcestershire sauce

3 dashes of Louisiana Red (page 18) or a bottled Louisiana-style sauce such as Tabasco

Pinch of salt

Pinch of ground celery seed

1 turn of freshly ground black pepper

Celery stalk

Pour vodka, V-8 juice, lemon juice, Worcestershire sauce, Tabasco, salt, and celery seed in a tall glass over ice. Decorate with black pepper and celery stalk.

Makes 1 drink.

The Starboard Restaurant in Dewey Beach, Delaware, has a collection of 1,600 hot sauces—50 of which are available for tasting on any given day. The most exotic? A Portuguese hot sauce from a Zulu tribe in South Africa. Anyone who brings in a new sauce gets a free meal, and on weekends customers can select from more than 300 hot sauces at the Bloody Mary smorgasbord.

PRAIRIE FIRE

Simple and to the point, this spirited drink appeals to many senses—from the smell of aged oak to the exquisite amber color to the flash of fire that pulses up to your ears and down to your belly. Been howling all night with the coyotes? For a Morning Praire Fire, add 2 shots of orange juice.

Cholula Hot Sauce
1 ounce Jose Cuervo Tequila

Shake a few dashes of hot sauce into a shot glass. Fill with tequila. Serve.

Makes 1 drink.

DEVILISH DAIQUIRI

Legend has it that this drink was named after a small, coastal village in Cuba where Americans landed in the 1890s after the Spanish-American war. The drink was later immortalized by Hemingway, who wrote in *Islands in the Stream* that the daiquiri, "reminded him of the sea. The frapped part of the drink was like the wake of a ship and the clear part was the way the water looked when the bow cut it when you were in shallow water over the marl bottom. That was almost the exact color." While this daiquiri has a slightly darker tint than Hemingway's, it may prove equally inspiring.

> 2 ounces amber rum
> Juice of ½ lime
> 1 teaspoon light brown sugar
> Dash of Louisiana Red (page 18) or a bottled Louisiana-style sauce such as Chef Hans' Louisiana Hot Pepper Sauce

Combine ingredients in a shaker, shake, strain, and serve over cracked ice.

Makes 1 drink.

MOLOTOV COCKTAIL

As Bakunin once remarked, "Dynamite will set you free."

> 1 shot Russian vodka
> 5 dashes of Louisiana Red (page 18) or a bottled Louisiana-style sauce such as Sho Nuff

Place a bottle of Russian vodka in the freezer for at least 6 hours. (It will become thick and slow-pouring but will not freeze.) Shake the hot sauce into the bottom of a shot glass. Top off with the vodka.

Makes 1 drink.

APPETIZERS

TOMATO BRUSCHETTA

This rustic summer dish depends on the integrity of the ingredients—use the fruitiest green olive oil and the ripest garden tomatoes. This makes a beautiful appetizer, or a tasty lunch, especially when accompanied by a simple soup. For summer entertaining, I brush the bread with olive oil and garlic, then cook it on the grill as guests are gathered round. The smell of garlic is irresistible.

>   2 large, ripe tomatoes, finely chopped
>   3 tablespoons capers
>   3 tablespoons chopped fresh parsley
> 1½ tablespoons chopped scallions
>   1 teaspoon balsamic vinegar
>   2 teaspoons Pili Pili (page 49) or even a bottled Caribbean-style sauce
>   such as Jab-Jab
>   Salt and freshly ground black pepper to taste
>   A French baguette
>   Up to ½ cup olive oil
>   3 medium garlic cloves, minced

Combine tomatoes, capers, parsley, scallions, vinegar, and hot sauce in a medium bowl. Sprinkle with salt and pepper. Taste and adjust seasonings. Allow the flavors to blend for 15 minutes.

Cut the bread into 22, ¼-inch thick ovals. Heat olive oil on low in a large skillet. Sauté garlic for 1 minute, then toast bread on either side. (Or, brush bread with olive oil and garlic and then toast on the grill.) Arrange tomato mixture on top of the bread and serve immediately.

Makes 22 hors d'oeuvres.

QUICK DIPS

The heat of a dip is a personal thing, so taste often as you add hot sauce to these effortless hors d'oeuvres:

* Combine a small packet of softened cream cheese, 2 tablespoons chutney, 2 teaspoons sour cream, and a few teaspoons of F-16 (page 27) or a bottled Caribbean-style hot sauce such as Yucatan Sunshine. Spread thinly on crackers and serve.

* Combine 3 parts chopped fresh tomatoes, 1 part diced bell peppers, 1 part diced red onion, and toss with Pebre (page 44) and serve with tortilla chips.

* Mix ¾ cup ketchup, 3 tablespoons of horseradish, a squirt of lemon, and a few dashes of Louisiana Red (page 18) or a bottled Louisiana-style sauce for an easy shrimp cocktail dip.

* In a real hurry? Buy a jar of mild salsa and add chopped green bell pepper and your favorite hot sauce for customized heat.

GUACAMOLE

While most Americans know guacamole as a chip dip, it's more traditionally served as a side dish for grilled meats. The secret of this dish is the balance between the cool avocado and the hot sauce, so taste often as you add the heat. The Louisiana hot sauce offers immediate, front-of-the-mouth heat, whereas the West Indian Pepper Sauce kicks in moments later—after you've savored the avocados, garlic, and lime—and provides a nice gustatory rif.

 4 *medium-ripe Haas avocados*
 2 *tablespoons fresh lime juice*
 ¼ *teaspoon salt*
 3 *medium garlic cloves, finely chopped*
 ½ *medium red onion, finely chopped*
 1 *medium tomato, chopped*
 1 *teaspoon Louisiana Red (page 18) or a bottled Louisiana-style sauce such as Louisiana Original Hot Sauce*
 2 *teaspoons West Indian Pepper Sauce (page 22) or a bottled Caribbean-style sauce such as Trinidad Habañero Pepper Sauce*

In a bowl, mash the avocados and lime juice with a fork, leaving some chunkiness. Stir in the remaining ingredients. Adjust seasoning. Serve within several hours at room temperature.

Makes 2 cups.

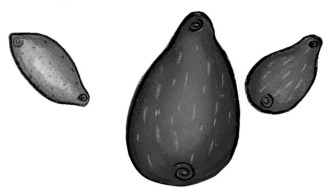

PITA TOASTS

Pita toasts are tasty as a light hors d'oeuvre or as a weight-conscious alternative to bread with dinner.

>   4   *(6-inch) pita breads*
>   4   *tablespoons butter*
>   *Harissa (page 45) or a bottled specialty sauce such as Clancy's*
>   *Fancy*
>   *Dried basil to taste*

Light broiler. Cut pitas into quarters and split open. Lightly butter the inside of each pita, then sprinkle with a few drops of hot sauce, smoothing the sauce thinly over the surface with a knife. Sprinkle with basil. Broil pitas butter side up until lightly toasted, about 3 minutes.

Serves 4.

Sambet's Cajun Store in Austin, Texas, features a hot sauce tasting bar with over 265 varieties, some of which will "take the top of your socks off," according to manager Jack Krc. With names like Bubba's Suicide Salsa, some are positively lethal. Watching my husband eye a flammable-looking brand, Krc quipped, "That one I wouldn't let you taste unless you've been there before."

Hot sauce tastings at home with friends can be fun, especially as your collection grows. In the summertime, we invite friends over and set out a few dozen bottles, along with tortilla chips and a few mild salsas for tasting. The table turns into a conversation piece, with people examining the labels and sampling the scorchers. When dinner is served (a mild dish like hamburgers), guests pick their own sauces for seasoning. Be sure to offer cooling accents—plenty of beer, a crisp green salad, and something fruity for dessert.

BLACK BEAN DIP

Black beans are popular in Cuba (where they're served on rice and referred to as "Moors and Christians"), and form the base for many delicious soups and entrees. They're also a natural companion to habañero-based hot sauces, especially since habañero means "from Havana," the legendary home of this king of chiles. The dense taste and rich chocolate color of the beans is a fabulous counter to the fruity spiciness of habañero sauces. Serve this tasty hors d'oeuvre with tortilla chips or pita toasts (recipe above) accompanied by a small bowl of ripe tomatoes, coarsely chopped and seasoned with freshly ground black pepper.

  1 *can (16-ounces) cooked black beans, rinsed and drained*
  1 *small ripe tomato*
  ½ *red bell pepper*
  1 *small red onion*
  2 *medium garlic cloves*
  1½ *tablespoon Chipotle Red Sauce (page 34) or a bottled border sauce such as Coyote Cocina Smoky Chipotle Sauce*
  1½ *tablespoons F-16 (page 27) or a bottled Caribbean-style sauce such as Busha Browne's Pukka Sauce*
  2 *tablespoons minced cilantro*
  1 *cup grated Monterey Jack or cheddar cheese (optional)*
  2 *tablespoons chopped scallion or cilantro*

In a blender or food processor combine the beans, tomato, bell pepper, onion, garlic, hot sauces, and cilantro. Process until smooth yet slightly chunky. Scoop bean puree into a saucepan and cook over low heat until hot, about 10 minutes. Stir in the cheese, if desired, and cook until cheese is melted. Serve immediately, garnished with scallion.

Serves 6.

SUMMER SALSA DEL FUEGO

Made in minutes, fresh salsa is not only a great dip, but a colorful accompaniment to grilled fish or chicken. The quality of the tomatoes will determine the success of the dish, so hunt for the best. Depending on your guests' attitudes, you might add a little less hot sauce, but keep a few bottles handy so the hotheads will be happy, too.

> 5 *large ripe tomatoes, coarsely chopped*
> 2 *teaspoons fresh lime juice*
> 1 *large garlic clove, minced*
> 1 *scallion, chopped*
> 1 *tablespoon olive oil*
> ½ *jalapeño chile, stemmed and finely chopped*
> 2 *tablespoons chopped cilantro*
> *Salt and freshly ground black pepper to taste*
> 1 *tablespoon West Indian Pepper Sauce (page 22) or a bottled*
>   *Caribbean-style sauce such as Island Treasure*

Combine all ingredients in a bowl and mix well.
Makes 2 cups.

BUFFALO CHICKEN WINGS

It was 1964 at the Anchor Bar in Buffalo and Theresa Bellissimo was at the grill when her son and his friends came in looking for something to eat. She deep fried the leftover chicken parts, shook them with hot sauce, then served them with celery and blue cheese on the side, and the famous wings were born. (Theresa, by the way, was married to Frank, of "Frank's Original" hot sauce.) The Anchor Bar lives on, where most customers order wings, along with "poppers" (deep-fried jalapeños coated with cheddar cheese). If you're not planning to shuffle off to Buffalo soon, try this great finger food.

> 2½ pounds (about 15) chicken wings
>   Vegetable oil for frying
> ¼ cup Louisiana Red (page 18) or a bottled Louisiana-style sauce such
>   as Crystal Extra Hot or ¾ cup Frank's Original RedHot
> 8 tablespoons butter, melted

Split wings at each joint, discarding tips. Pat dry. Heat oil to 375 degrees and deep fry until crispy and cooked. Shake in a brown paper bag to drain the oil.

In a large bowl, combine hot sauce and butter. Dip wings into sauce to coat completely. (If wings are too hot, add more butter; if they're too mild, add more hot sauce.)

Makes 15 wings.

Variation: Bake wings in a 425 degree oven for 1 hour, turning them after 30 minutes.

SPICY GRILLED SHIITAKES
WITH GINGER AND GARLIC

With their firm, beef-like texture and woodsy flavor, shiitakes are delicious grilled. For appetizers, I select mid-sized shiitakes (3 to 4 inches in diameter), whereas if I'm serving this as a side dish I opt for smaller shiitakes, or—to make a dramatic gesture—I go for the giant ones, which remind me of the grilled porcinis I've seen served in Tuscany.

> 1 pound Delftree shiitake mushrooms (see note), stems removed
>
> 4 teaspoons minced fresh ginger
>
> 6 large garlic cloves, minced
>
> 5 tablespoons soy sauce
>
> ¼ cup dry sherry
>
> ½ cup peanut oil
>
> 4 tablespoons Spicy Island Hot Sauce (page 20) or a bottled
>   Caribbean-style sauce such as Evadney's Jamaican Hot Sauce

In a large bowl, whisk together the ginger, garlic, soy sauce, sherry, peanut oil, and hot sauce. Add the mushrooms and toss thoroughly to combine. Set aside to marinate 30 to 45 minutes, tossing occasionally.

Prepare a grill. Grill the whole mushroom caps until they are tender and slightly crispy, about 3 to 5 minutes per side, depending on the thickness of the mushrooms. Serve hot.

Serves 6.

Note: Although any fresh shiitakes are suitable, I prefer Delftree shiitakes, which are organically grown and shipped to you within 48 hours of being picked. (See Mail-Order Sources.)

Return of the Devilled Egg

The devil likes it hot, and "devilled" foods are traditionally those seasoned with a piquant sauce often spiked with cayenne. Devilled eggs have become weak versions of what they are meant to be, and this recipe restores the zest that gave them their name.

> 5 *eggs*
> 3 *tablespoons mayonnaise*
> 1 *teaspoon dry mustard*
> 4 *teaspoons Harissa (page 45) or even a bottled Caribbean-style sauce such as Jamaica Hell Fire*
> 1 *teaspoon curry powder*
> 1 *tablespoon chopped fresh basil*

Put the eggs in a medium saucepan and cover with cold water. Bring the water to a boil, then lower heat and simmer for 10 minutes. Drain the eggs and cover with cold water. Peel when cool.

Cut the eggs in half lengthwise and remove the yolks. In a small bowl, use a fork to mash the yolks with the mayonnaise, mustard, 2 teaspoons of the hot sauce, curry, and basil. Mix well and mound the filling into the whites. Top each egg with a dab of Harissa.

Makes 10 hors d'oeuvres.

Barnacle Ban

Ken Fisher experienced the heat late in life, but when he did, it was like a visit from the mother of invention herself. He recalled later, "I ate that devilled egg, and my eyes began to water, my nose ran, my forehead broke out in sweat, and I thought, there ought to be *something* this stuff is good for." In a quantum leap, Ken's mind jumped from hot sauce to barnacles, which he had been fighting for years on his Florida fishing boat. "If hot sauce did that to me," he said, "I figured it would do the same to barnacles." His experiments led to a new line of boat paint called Barnacle Ban, which contains cayenne. And it works!

CREOLE PUMPKIN SOUP

At the Sugar Mill Hotel, built on the grounds of a 350-year-old sugar mill in Tortola, I was served this soup whose delicate flavors were accented by the unmistakable presence of hot sauce. Inquiring, I learned that chef Jeff Oakley often used hot sauce made down the road by the Sunny Caribbee. In making this soup, balancing the flavors is important, so add the hot sauce a little at a time and taste often.

1 *medium yellow onion, diced*
4 *medium garlic cloves, minced*
1 *stalk celery, diced*
2 *medium carrots, diced*
2 *tablespoons vegetable oil*
4 *tablespoons brown sugar*
1 *teaspoon nutmeg*

5 cups chicken stock

3 cups fresh West Indian pumpkin (see Note), cut into 1" cubes

½ cup smooth peanut butter

1 cup heavy cream

3 tablespoons fresh lime juice

1½ tablespoons West Indian Pepper Sauce (page 22) or a bottled
    Caribbean-style sauce such as Sunny Caribbee

Salt and freshly ground pepper to taste

Toasted pumpkin seeds (optional garnish)

Sour cream (optional garnish)

In a heavy pot, sauté onion, garlic, celery, and carrots in oil until they're soft. Stir in sugar and nutmeg. Add chicken stock and pumpkin and cook until pumpkin is soft. Puree ingredients in a blender and return to pot. Bring to a simmer and stir in peanut butter, cream, lime juice, and hot sauce. Add salt and pepper, and more hot sauce if desired. (If a thinner soup is desired, add more chicken stock or water.) Garnish with toasted pumpkin seeds or sour cream.

Serves 4 to 6.

Note: West Indian pumpkin (or calabaza) is a yellow pumpkin-like squash found in Caribbean and Latin American markets. While West Indian pumpkin is preferred because of its color and flavor, substitutes include other pumpkins, or Hubbard or butternut squash.

Soups and hot sauce were made for each other. A few drops will spike up ratatouille, vichyssoise, oyster stew, fish chowder, as well as pea or bean soups. You might start with a pique, work up to a hot pepper sherry, and then venture on to sauces with cayenne and habañero chiles.

GAZPACHO

This spicy version of the classic Spanish soup has a nice zip but is not "wicked hot" as they say where I come from. This is a dish suitable for many garden vegetables; you can substitute fresh chives or basil for the parsley, or add another bell pepper. You can also dice the onion or—as Alice B. Toklas recommended in her *Cookery Book*—cut it as "thin as tissue paper."

 2 ripe tomatoes, peeled, seeded, and finely chopped

 1 red or green bell pepper, diced

 2 medium garlic cloves, minced

 ½ teaspoon salt

 ¼ cup chopped parsley

 ⅓ cup extra-virgin olive oil

 2 teaspoons balsamic vinegar

 3 cups V-8 or tomato juice

 2 tablespoons Death Wish (page 47) or a bottled specialty sauce such as Lotta Hotta Besos de Fuego

 ½ medium red onion, finely chopped

 2 medium cucumbers, peeled, seeded, and grated

 1 cup croutons

Combine the tomatoes, bell pepper, garlic, salt, and parsley in a bowl. Stir in the oil, vinegar, tomato juice, and hot sauce. Taste and adjust heat level. Add onion and cucumbers and mix well. Serve chilled, each bowl topped with croutons.

Serves 4.

SPICY PAPPARDELLE WITH
SUMMER TOMATOES, CUCUMBERS, AND BASIL

I have been known to make a 3-hour detour to eat at Johanne Killeen and George Germon's Al Forno restaurant in Providence, Rhode Island. Certainly two of the country's best chefs, they are known for their use of marvelously fresh ingredients cooked in a spirited style, which you will taste immediately in this wonderful pasta dish of theirs.

> 4 small, vine-ripened tomatoes, cored and chopped
>
> 4 Kirby (pickling) cucumbers, skin on, coarsely chopped
>
> 1–2 teaspoons West Indian Pepper Sauce (page 22) or a bottled Caribbean-style sauce such as Melinda's, or more to taste
>
> ½ cup virgin olive oil
>
> 2 teaspoons red wine vinegar
>
> 1–2 teaspoons kosher (sea) salt
>
> 8 ounces imported pappardelle
>
> ¼ cup chopped fresh, Italian flat-leaf parsley
>
> 6 leaves fresh basil, cut into a chiffonade just before using

In a large serving bowl, combine the tomatoes, cucumbers, hot sauce, olive oil, vinegar, and salt. Allow to sit at room temperature for ½ hour for flavors to combine.

Bring a large pot of salted water to boil. Boil the pappardelle until al dente (4–5 minutes), drain, and toss in the bowl with the remaining ingredients. Serve immediately.

Serves 4 to 6 (or 2 as a main course).

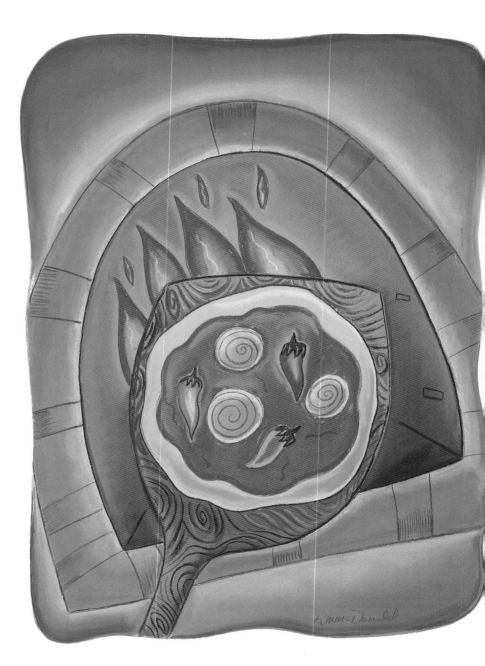

MAIN COURSES

SPICY PIZZA WITH BLACK OLIVADA AND SMOKY SALSA PICANTE

To make terrific pizzas at home with crispy crusts, you need two tools well worth the investment: a baking stone and a flat wooden paddle known as a pizza peel. Beyond that, choose a fruity olive oil—the best you can afford—and you're on your way. I've listed below many options for pizza toppings—we often invite a few friends over, set out the many pizza toppings, and let things unfold from there. (To make this an easy meal, I use fresh or frozen pizza dough prepared by my supermarket bakery.)

1 pound frozen pizza dough
4 tablespoons olive oil

OPTIONAL TOPPING COMBINATIONS

Black olivada (see note)
Green olivada
A bottled border sauce such as Santa Fe Exotix Green Chile Sauce
Smoky Salsa Picante (page 32), Chipotle Red Sauce (page 34), or
    any of several bottled border sauces such as La Gloria Chipotle
    Sauce
Sun-dried tomatoes, thinly sliced
1 dried ancho chile, stemmed, seeded, and thinly sliced
Fresh garlic, thinly sliced or minced
Red onion, thinly sliced
Sliced calamata olives
Anchovies
Freshly shaved fontina cheese
Freshly shaved mozzarella cheese
Freshly grated Romano or Parmesan cheese
Fresh rosemary, thyme, basil, or oregano
Freshly ground black pepper

The night before cooking, place the frozen dough in the refrigerator to thaw. A few hours before eating, place the thawed dough in a bowl, brush the top surface with a thin layer of olive oil, cover with plastic wrap, and allow to rise in a warm place for 2 hours.

Put stone on lower rack of oven and preheat oven to 500 degrees. Dust the wooden spatula with corn meal, which allows the pizza to slide off the spatula with ease. On a well-floured surface, roll and stretch half of the dough cracker thin. (It should be thin enough that you can see light through it, and it's okay if small tears form.) Place the stretched dough on the spatula and finish pulling and shaping the pizza dough on the board.

Brush the top of the dough with a thin layer of olive oil. Spread any number of toppings on the dough. Some combinations include black olivada, a border sauce, and black pepper; Smoky Salsa Picante, minced garlic, mozzarella, and black pepper; mozzarella, Romano, sun-dried tomatoes, and Chipotle Red Sauce.

With a quick motion, shimmy the pizza onto the baking stone and cook until lightly browned, about 12 minutes. Slice and serve immediately. Repeat for the next pizza.

Makes 2 medium pizzas.

Note: Olivada, a commercially prepared puree of olives, herbs, and olive oil, is available in most gourmet stores.

Suggested Wine: A dry red Italian, such as Montepulciano D'Abruzzo, or a good 1990 Chianti such as Le Bocce Classico.

"Red beans and ricely yours"
—the way Louis Armstrong signed his letters.

RED BEANS AND RICE

When my husband and I are in Vieques, where fresh produce and meats aren't always readily available, we often make a big batch of beans in the morning, then leave it to simmer on the stove and head to the beach. This dish is intentionally quite mild: beans and rice are the ultimate foil for hot sauces. If you're having friends over, serve with a green salad, crusty hot bread, and a dozen or so lively bottled hot sauces as your centerpiece.

    1 pound red kidney beans, rinsed
    ¼ cup olive oil
    1 large yellow onion, coarsely chopped
    4 large garlic cloves, minced
    ½ cup chopped pimentos
    1 stalk celery, chopped
    ⅓ cup rum
    ⅓ cup cilantro leaves (packed), finely chopped
    ¼ teaspoon cumin seeds
    2 teaspoons F-16 (page 27) or a bottled Caribbean-style sauce such as
       Mrs. Dog's
    6 cups hot, cooked white rice

Soak beans overnight in enough water to cover as they expand.

In a large kettle over medium heat, heat the olive oil and sauté onions and garlic until translucent, about 8 minutes. Drain the beans and add to kettle, along with the remaining ingredients, except the rice. Bring to a boil, then simmer 4 to 5 hours, or until beans are soft and liquid is thick but still sauce-like, adding water every hour or so if necessary. Adjust seasonings and serve on plates over hot rice, along with several hot sauce bottles so guests can customize the spiciness of their dish.

Serves 6.

SUGGESTED WINE: Lots of any good quality jug wine, like Phillip's Night Harvest Red (a Rhone-style blend), or Rene Juno Rouge, Mirassou Zinfandel, Monterey Vineyard Red.

SEAFOOD STEW, WEST INDIES STYLE

This recipe comes from Chris Schlesinger, a man who knows spicy food and live coals, and demonstrates it nightly at the East Coast Grill, one of the best restaurants in Boston. He also happens to make one of my favorite hot sauces, Inner Beauty. "Use Inner Beauty to enhance dull and boring food," Chris advises. "Keep away from pets, open flames and bad advice. This is not a toy. This is serious. Stand up straight, sit right, and stop mumbling." Amen. This delicious stew has the perfect amount of heat; it adds interest without burning and is something of a surprise.

½ pound medium shrimp, peeled and deveined

12 medium sea scallops

1 10-ounce mackerel or kingfish fillet

1 8- to 10-ounce spiny lobster tail, shelled (available frozen in supermarkets)

3 tablespoons vegetable oil

2 large yellow onions, finely chopped

3 stalks celery, finely chopped

2 tablespoons minced garlic

1 cup white wine

1½ quarts bottled clam juice

½ teaspoon ground cumin

¼ teaspoon allspice

2 large sweet potatoes, scrubbed clean and cut into large cubes

½ pound fresh okra, stems removed, cut into thick rounds

2 fresh tomatoes, coarsely chopped

   Salt and freshly ground pepper to taste

4 tablespoons fresh lime juice

3 tablespoons chopped cilantro

2 tablespoons Pineapple Curry Heat Wave (page 26) or a bottled Caribbean-style sauce such as Inner Beauty Real Hot Sauce

Over a hot fire, grill each kind of seafood separately. The shrimp will take approximately 3 to 4 minutes per side, the scallops 3 minutes per side, the mackerel 5 minutes per side, and the lobster 4 minutes per side. As each is done, remove it from grill and set aside. (Note: you want the seafood to get some surface color; don't worry too much about cooking it completely, as it will finish in the broth.)

In a large saucepan or soup pot, heat the oil over medium heat until very hot but not smoking. Sauté the onion and celery until clear, about 5 minutes. Add the garlic and sauté an additional minute. Add the wine, clam juice, cumin, and allspice and bring to a simmer. Add the sweet potato, okra, and tomato and continue to simmer for 30 minutes.

Add any of the seafood that is not completely cooked and simmer for 4 minutes. Just before serving, add the remaining seafood and simmer for 1 minute, just to warm it through. Remove the pot from the heat and add the salt and pepper. Just before serving, toss in the lime juice, cilantro, and hot sauce.

Serves 8.

Suggested Wine: A sauvignon blanc from California's Groth or Sanford Vineyards, or New Zealand's Stoneleigh Vineyards. A quality Stout such as Samuel Smith's Oatmeal Stout would also be good.

Fresh, ripe papayas sliced open, seeded, and sprinkled with lime juice make a delicious cooling dessert after a spicy meal.

Go Big Red

Raised in the Oklahoma Panhandle, my husband makes a great bowl of chili, which includes both tomatoes and beans—something chili diehards south of the Oklahoma border would likely omit. Joe's chili is hot but not a scorcher; you can control the heat by varying the amount of chili powder added, depending on your heat predilection and chili source. Serve it with corn bread, green salad, and beer—and always on big football days.

- ½ cup olive oil plus 1 teaspoon
- 2 medium yellow onions, coarsely chopped
- 1 pound hot sausage meat (loose ground, or links with casings removed)
- 1 pound lean, ground beef
- 2 bottles (12 ounces each) beer
- 1 can (28 ounces) plum tomatoes with their juices
- 2–3 tablespoons pure chili powder or 4 tablespoons commercial blend (see box)
- 1 tablespoon whole cumin seeds
- 1 tablespoon dried oregano
- ½ teaspoon ginger
- 1 teaspoon salt
- ¼ teaspoon ground allspice
- 1 cup water
- 1 can (15 ounces) light red kidney beans, rinsed and drained
- 1 can (15 ounces) dark red kidney beans, rinsed and drained
- 6 large garlic cloves, finely chopped
- 4 teaspoons West Indian Pepper Sauce (page 22) or a bottled Caribbean-style sauce such as D. L. Jardine's Blazin' Saddle, or 2 teaspoons Death Wish (page 47) for a redder color

  Sour cream or grated Longhorn cheese (optional garnish)

  Sliced Haas avocado (optional garnish)

Heat oil in a large soup pot over medium heat. Add onions and cook, stirring occasionally, until translucent to golden, about 10 minutes.

In a separate skillet, heat the remaining teaspoon of oil over medium heat, crumble in the sausage and beef, and cook, stirring often, until sausage and beef lose their pinkness, about 8 minutes. Spoon out excess fat.

Transfer the sausage and beef to the pot with the onions, and turn flame to low. Add the beer (minus a swig for yourself) and the tomatoes with their juices, breaking up the tomatoes with a knife. Stir in the chili powder, cumin, oregano, ginger, salt, and allspice. Add the water and simmer, covered, for 1½ hours. Add beans and garlic and simmer until done, about 30 minutes to 1 hour, stirring occasionally. Add hot sauce just before serving or put a bottle of hot sauce on the table and let people add their own. You might garnish with sour cream and sliced avocado—though Joe takes his straight up.

Serves 4 to 6.

Note: Chili is good served immediately, and even better refrigerated overnight and reheated the next day.

Chili Powder

Those who use chili powder daily often prefer a pure ground chili powder to the commercial ones, which are actually blends of dried chiles, black pepper, salt, sugar, oregano, cumin, and garlic powder. The taste of pure chili powder is sharper, with a slightly bitter edge. Using the pure form allows you to control how much cumin and other ingredients you add to your dish. Besides, the color of pure, ground chili is gorgeous—a deep vermillion red reminiscent of the Southwestern countryside itself.

FAJITAS

Devised as a way to make skirt steak palatable to ranch hands working along the Rio Grande, fajitas are now so popular that upscale cookbooks list skirt steak as one of the best cuts. In reality, skirt steak is a fancy name for the tough cut located approximately where you might find your love handles, and is much improved by marinating, then cutting against the grain into thin strips (or fajitas, which means "little belts" in Spanish). Though the skirt cut is most authentic, I prefer flank steak, which is less gristly and easier to find at the store. Colorful and fun to make, fajitas are a real crowd pleaser—and something that kids generally love. With the fillings served buffet-style, it's also a great way to show off your hot sauce collection.

½ cup plus 2 tablespoons olive oil
6 tablespoons Smoky Salsa Picante (page 32)
3 tablespoons fresh lime juice
1½ pound beef skirt steak or flank steak (London broil)
 Handful of mesquite chips (optional)
1 dozen flour tortillas

FILLINGS

1 large Vidalia onion, diced
1 green or red bell pepper, thinly sliced
 Sour cream
 Sliced avocadoes or Guacamole (page 60)
 Chopped tomatoes or Summer Salsa del Fuego (page 63)
 Shredded lettuce
 Smoky Salsa Picante (page 32), or a bottled border sauce such as
  El Yucateco Red
1 lime, cut into thin wedges
 Fresh chopped mint

Combine ½ cup of the oil, the picante, and the lime juice in a medium bowl. Add the steak, turn to coat and marinate for 1 to 24 hours, refrigerated.

Soak the mesquite chips in water for 30 minutes. Prepare grill, drain the mesquite chips and add to the coals just before cooking the steak. Grill steak until cooked medium rare, 6–7 minutes per side. Heat 2 tablespoons of oil in a large skillet on the stove, and sauté onion and pepper until somewhat soft, about 7 to 8 minutes.

To warm the tortillas, brush them with oil and put on grill for 20 seconds, then flip and allow to heat briefly on the other side. Or, for a slight crispness, put a teaspoon of vegetable oil in a skillet and heat the tortilla for 10 to 15 seconds on one side, then flip briefly to heat the other side. (Or, heat oven to 400 degrees and place on rack for 2 to 3 minutes.)

Slice the steak thinly at a 45-degree angle to the grain. Place on a large platter and serve with warm tortillas and various fillings, allowing people to mix and roll their own fajitas. Set out a small dish of lime wedges, so that everyone can top their concoctions with a squirt of lime.

Serves 4.

Mo Hotta Mo Betta

Can't find Dr. J's Chile Elixir? Call Mo Hotta Mo Betta, a mail-order company specializing in hot sauces and foods. In the lively catalog, you can follow the adventures of "Mo" and his pulsating palate, and order hundreds of hot sauces—from Lingham's Chilly Sauce (made in Malaysia since 1908) to Miz Grazi's Hot Stuff (a '30s Mississippi brew "almost as potent as moonshine"). And—for the chef who has everything—there's always Hot Nuts. (For Mail-Order Sources, see page 123.)

TANGY SKIRT STEAK TAMPIQUENO TACOS

These delicious tacos were created by Mark Miller and Mark Kiffin at the Coyote Cafe in Santa Fe, where some of this country's most inventive culinary work gets done. For this dish, the Coyote's bottled hot sauce is a perfect match with the poblano peppers and cilantro. Served with black beans and rice, this is a tasty lunch: for more spice, pour extra hot sauce over the finished tacos just before serving.

    2 pounds skirt or flank steak
    ¼ cup plus 1 tablespoon Chipotle Red Sauce (page 34) or ½ bottle
        Coyote Cocina's Tangy Taco Sauce
    5 tablespoons olive oil
    1¼ teaspoon salt
    1 medium white onion, chopped
    1 poblano chile, stemmed, cored, and chopped
    1 red bell pepper, stemmed, cored, and chopped
    1 dozen warm white or yellow corn tortillas
    ¼ cup fresh cilantro leaves

Marinate the whole steak with hot sauce, 2 tablespoons of the oil and 1 teaspoon of the salt. Let sit at room temperature for 1 hour. Grill steak over charcoal or under broiler until medium rare. Sauté the onions and peppers in 3 tablespoons oil, and season with ¼ teaspoon salt.

Slice steak in thin strips across the grain of the meat and place with pepper and onion mixture over tortillas. Garnish with fresh cilantro and fold to serve.

Serves 4.

SUGGESTED WINE: A lush Australian Shiraz from Brown Brothers, or a California Zinfandel from 1990 or 1991. The "Three Rs"—Ravenswood, Ridge, and Rafanelli—are all fine producers of Zinfandels. Beer is also a good match; try Pilsner Urquell.

"Chiles are a life-style"
—Mark Miller

On the Sante Fe Trail at 12,000 feet

I'd been married about 11 minutes when my husband, a new pilot with 50 hours in his logbook, suggested that we fly from Massachusetts to the Grand Canyon for our honeymoon. I of course said yes, and soon we were heading in a little Grumman Cheetah over the Santa Fe Trail. Flying over the pass of New Mexico's Sangre de Cristo Mountains, we followed the Rio Grande River to Santa Fe, which—while suffering from "Santa Fe Chic"—still is a marvelous place. Spanish, Native American, and Southwestern culinary styles converge in a unique way and are evident in everything from the honey-drenched sopaillas at Rancho de Chimayo to the Yucatan lamb with smoked chile sauce at the Coyote Cafe. While there, don't miss Coyote's general store, which features 200 hot sauces.

STATESBOROUGH MEATLOAF

The idea for this meatloaf occurred to me at a diner in Georgia, where I saw a man open up a meatloaf sandwich and douse it with hot sauce. I did the same, and it was delicious. This recipe is even better, because the hot sauce melds with the onion and garlic in the cooking process and adds spine and surprise to this comfort food. (The choice of hot sauce will regulate the heat—if you substitute a Louisiana hot sauce, it will be mild enough for kids.) It's delicious served hot, and a treat the next day tucked into a sandwich.

1½ tablespoons vegetable oil
1 medium onion, chopped
3 medium garlic cloves, crushed
2 pounds lean, ground beef
2 teaspoons salt
1 teaspoon black pepper
2 eggs, beaten
¾ cup V-8 or tomato juice
½ cup chopped fresh parsley
1 tablespoon Death Wish (page 47) or a bottled Caribbean-style
    sauce such as Hellfire & Damnation Hot Sauce
1 cup fresh breadcrumbs

Preheat oven to 350 degrees. Heat the oil in a skillet and sauté onion until translucent, about 5 minutes. Add garlic and sauté 1 minute. Transfer the onion and garlic into a large mixing bowl and add the beef, salt, black pepper, eggs, juice, parsley, and sauce. Mix well.

Oil a 12- x 8- x 2-inch pan and pour in mixture, molding it into a loaf. Sprinkle the top with breadcrumbs and bake for 1 hour.

Serves 6.

SUGGESTED WINE: A "Cru Beaujolais" such as Moulin-a-Vent or Saint Amour.

SOUTHERN MILK-FRIED CHICKEN

I first tasted this subtle peppery fried chicken at the Tanglewood Music Festival, when my future mother-in-law arrived with a wicker hamper laden with down-home Oklahoma goodies, including this delicious chicken, fresh biscuits, okra salad, and minty iced tea.

> 2 *cups milk*
> ¼ *cup Louisiana Red (page 18) or a bottled Louisiana-style sauce such as Dr. J's Habañero Chile Elixir*
> 1½ *teaspoons salt*
> 1 *medium frying chicken at room temperature, cut into serving pieces*
> 2 *cups unbleached, all-purpose flour*
> *Vegetable shortening or corn oil for frying*

Combine the milk, hot sauce, and ¾ teaspoon of the salt in a shallow casserole dish (it's ok if the milk curdles from the vinegar in the sauce). Add the chicken and marinate for 30 minutes, turning once after 15 minutes.

Meanwhile, combine the flour and remaining salt in a paper bag. Remove chicken from milk mixture and place in the bag a few pieces at a time. Shake until they are coated and place coated pieces on waxed paper.

Put ½-inch oil in large skillet and heat to 325 degrees. (Make sure it's not smoking.) Fry the chicken gently, covered, for 30 minutes, then turn chicken once. Replace lid, and fry chicken for 25 minutes more, or until golden brown and cripsy. Drain chicken on paper towels.

Serves 4.

SUGGESTED WINE: Carmenet's Old Vines Colombard, Chappelet Dry Chenin Blanc, or Columbia Crest Semillon/Chardonnay. An Alsatian Pinot Blanc would be a fine reasonably priced choice.

ROASTED PORK HABAÑERO

This dish is derived from traditional Caribbean roast pork recipes, substituting a habañero hot sauce for mashed red peppers in the marinade. The flavors of the sauce infuse deeply into the pork, giving the meat a remarkable complexity. With care, the pork can be grilled over low coals. However, this will require tending, for the meat drippings can flare up and char the pork, ruining the surprisingly delicate flavor of the marinade. I usually first sear the roast over a gas grill fed with a few hickory chips for a quick smoke and nicely browned surface, then finish it in the oven. This dish is good with steamed new potatoes and a fresh green vegetable.

> 1 (5-pound) leg or loin of pork
> 6 large garlic cloves, cut into long slivers
> 3 tablespoons Pineapple Curry Heat Wave (page 26) or a bottled
>   Caribbean-style sauce such as Matouk's Calypso Sauce
> ¼ cup fresh lime juice
> 3 cups sherry
> 1 teaspoon oregano
> 1 teaspoon ground coriander
> 1 bay leaf
> 1 teaspoon salt
> 3 tablespoons olive oil
> ½ cup cracked green olives, sliced and pitted
> ½ cup black, Greek olives, sliced and pitted

With a sharp knife, stab deep cuts into the pork, and stud with garlic slivers. Place pork in a bowl suitable for marinating.

Combine hot sauce, lime juice, and 2 cups of sherry with oregano, coriander, bay leaf, salt, and 1 tablespoon of the oil. Pour over the pork, rubbing into the knife cuts, and let stand covered and refrigerated for 24 hours, turning several times or basting.

Return pork to room temperature. Preheat oven to 325 degrees. In a heavy casserole dish large enough to hold roast, heat remaining oil over medium heat and brown meat all over. (Or, place the roast on a grill and brown over medium fire, about 15 minutes, adding hickory chips to smoke it, if desired.)

Remove roast from stove, cover with a tight-fitting lid, and roast the pork in its marinade for 3 hours, or until done, basting every half hour. (Most people still prefer pork well done, or when the meat thermometer reads 180 degrees.) Transfer pork to platter.

Place the casserole dish and remaining juices on the stove top, add olives and 1 cup of sherry, and cook over medium heat. Stir often until reduced slightly. Slice the pork, and serve with sauce and olives drizzled over the slices.

Serves 6 to 8.

SUGGESTED WINE: A French burgundy, or a more affordable French pinot noir such as the French Faiveley or Louis Jadot, or Saintsbury from California or Elk Cove Vineyards from Oregon.

GRILL CRAZY

Some easy favorites

* Four boneless chicken breasts, marinated in ⅓ cup of Joe's Soak Sauce (page 38) for several hours, then grilled.

* Pork chops marinated for several hours in Pineapple Curry Heat Wave (page 26) or a bottled Caribbean-style sauce, such as Sontava, with a pinch of oregano and minced garlic, then grilled.

* Chicken marinated in Hatch Special (page 39), olive oil, and garlic, then stir-fried.

* Bite-sized beef kebabs seasoned with salt and pepper, then marinated for an hour in 1 part olive oil and 3 parts Smoky Salsa Picante (page 32) or a bottled Caribbean-style sauce such as Salu's, then skewered and grilled.

GRILLED HOT THIGHS

I love jerk, which I learned not in Jamaica, but on Cape Cod, where a sailing buddy regaled me for the better part of a day with what he'd learned in the islands. I usually don't have time to do the jerk justice, however, and instead use this shortcut, which is fantastic for the grill (and like the jerk, has hot peppers as its soul). The flavor of the habañeros in the hot sauce will survive the rigors of the grill, as will the other ingredients, all chosen for their strength and robustness.

- 8 chicken thighs
- 5 tablespoons Spicy Island Hot Sauce (page 20) or a bottled Caribbean-style sauce such as Dat'l Do-it Hot Sauce
- 2 medium garlic cloves, minced
- ½ teaspoon salt
- 2 tablespoons fresh lime juice
- ¼ cup rum
  - ½-inch piece ginger root, finely chopped
- ½ tablespoon coarse mustard
- 1 tablespoon balsamic vinegar
- 1 tablespoon olive oil

Rinse chicken and dry with a paper towel. Place in a nonmetallic bowl. Combine remaining ingredients and pour over chicken. Marinate in the refrigerator for 3 hours.

Prepare grill. Return chicken to room temperature. Grill chicken over medium coals for about 30 minutes, turning the pieces after 15 minutes and basting them frequently. The chicken should have a nice, browned surface. The thighs are done when the juices flow clear. Serve immediately, or cold as picnic fare.

Serves 3 to 4.

SUGGESTED WINE: A Northern Italian Pinot Grigio or wines from Cavit, Torresella, and Santa Margarita.

SMOKED SPARERIBS

The first secret to good ribs is slow cooking, preferably in a covered grill large enough so that the ribs do not sit over live coals but are off to the side. The second secret is to use a spicy, vinegar-based marinade such as Joe's Soak Sauce (page 38). If you have a large, covered grill—or, better yet, a good smoke pit—be sure to fire it with hardwood charcoal, adding hickory or mesquite chips just before you put the meat on. If you're using a two-burner gas grill, light it on one side only. Otherwise, you can follow the alternative oven-cooking technique below to get a good approximation of authentic barbecue.

> 2 (3-pound) racks of spareribs, brisket flaps still attached
> 4 cups Joe's Soak Sauce (page 38) or Rozelene's Barbecue Baste &
>   Marinade from the Stonewall Chili Pepper Company
> 1 cup mesquite chips, soaked in water ½ hour
> 1 cup Hot Smoke Finishing Sauce (page 36) or bottled barbecue
>   sauce of choice

Marinate the ribs in the soak sauce for 3 to 6 hours, refrigerated, turning or basting frequently.

Barbecue technique

Using hardwood charcoal, set a fire under half a covered grill. When coals have begun to burn evenly, toss the mesquite chips onto the coals, place the ribs on the cool end of the grate (not directly over the coals), and cover. Check ribs after 15 minutes to ensure that the cooking is not proceeding too quickly. If the ribs are sizzling or beginning to show signs of browning, control heat by moving ribs farther from fire, spreading the coals, or removing the cover, allowing the coals to burn down somewhat. Turn and baste ribs every 30 minutes, and continue cooking for about 2½ hours, or until done. (You can test for doneness by splitting a rack.) Serve with Hot Smoke Finishing Sauce, coleslaw, corn on the cob, and beer.

Oven technique

Preheat oven to 200 degrees. Place marinated ribs on foil-covered cookie sheets, and cook for 2½ hours, turning and basting once.

Prepare grill. Remove ribs from oven. Just before eating, baste them once more with Joe's Soak Sauce and place them on grill directly over medium coals for about 6 minutes per side. During the last minute of cooking on each side, brush on the Hot Smoke Finishing Sauce and serve with more of the Finishing Sauce on the side.

Serves 4 to 6.

Too Darned Hot

Hot sauce got your tongue? The best cool-down remedy is to drink a half cup of milk. Other dairy products (ice cream, yogurt, sour cream) also provide relief, as do starches (bread, potatoes, rice). Beer, on the other hand, fans the flames, acting as a dispersant. But I still prefer it to milk.

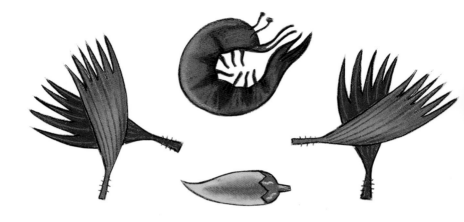

SHRIMP AND TASSO WITH FIVE-PEPPER JELLY

This recipe comes from chef Jaimie Shannon at Commander's Palace, a New Orleans institution dating back to 1880. Though this dish is a multi-part affair requiring a bit of preparation, the result is magnificent. Do not omit the pickled okra—their crisp, sour bite brings out a delicate sweetness you would otherwise miss, and nestled between the shrimp atop a colorful bed of pepper relish, they help create a baroque visual effect that will remind you of New Orleans and Mardi Gras.

FIVE-PEPPER JELLY

> 4 tablespoons honey
> ½ cup plus 2 tablespoons white vinegar
> 1 red bell pepper, cored and diced

1 green bell pepper, cored and diced

1 yellow bell pepper, cored and diced

1 jalapeño pepper, cored and diced

¼ teaspoon black pepper

Salt to taste

SHRIMP AND TASSO

24 jumbo shrimp, shelled and deveined

¼ pound spicy tasso, julienned into 1-inch strips

1 cup flour (seasoned with 5 or 6 turns of peppermill)

2 cups vegetable or peanut oil

4 tablespoons Crystal Hot Butter (see next page)

24 pickled okra

To prepare the pepper jelly, combine honey and vinegar in a pot and reduce until it is sticky. Add peppers and black pepper and cook until peppers are soft. Add salt to taste.

To cook the shrimp, make a ¼-inch incision down the back of each shrimp, and place one strip of tasso in each incision, securing with a toothpick. Lightly dust each shrimp with flour. In a 12-inch skillet, heat oil until hot but not smoking. Fry about 2 minutes per side, or until shrimp lose their translucence. Remove to paper towel to drain, then place cooked shrimp in a bowl and toss with hot-sauce butter until well coated.

Spread Five-Pepper Jelly on the bottom of the serving platter. Arrange the shrimp and okra over the jelly in an alternating fashion.

Serves 4.

SUGGESTED WINE: Complex flavors would make a Meursault or Puligny-Montrachet from Louis Latour or Olivier Leflaive work its magic. A Reserve Gewurztraminer from Alsace would be great, or a California chardonnay such as Cambria "Katherine's Vineyard."

CRYSTAL HOT BUTTER

Delicious with bread, or drizzled over green vegetables, this hot butter will jazz up almost anything.

½ medium garlic clove, minced
1 teaspoon shallots, minced
½ pound butter, softened
¼ cup plus 1 tablespoon Crystal or other Louisiana hot sauce
1 tablespoon heavy cream

Sauté garlic and shallots in a pan with 1 tablespoon of the butter. Add the hot sauce and reduce by 75%. Add cream and reduce by 50%. Remove from heat, and in a separate bowl, slowly whip in the softened butter a little at a time. Refrigerate until using.

BARBECUE SPICED SHRIMP

This is a great summer dish, and if you're serving it at an outdoor party, you might let guests put their own shrimp on the grill on an ad hoc basis.

4 tablespoons olive oil
6 tablespoons Pebre (page 44) or a bottled specialty sauce such as Craig's Hot Pepper Sauce
2 medium garlic cloves, minced
2 teaspoons fresh lime juice
50 medium shrimp, shelled and deveined

Combine olive oil, hot sauce, garlic, and lime and mix well. Add shrimp, stir to coat, and allow mixture to stand for an hour.

Light the grill. Thread the shrimp onto skewers and grill over medium heat, 2 to 3 minutes per side. Remove from heat and serve immediately.

Serves 4 (or 10 as an hors d'oeuvre).

SUGGESTED WINE: An Australian chardonnay such as Oxford Landing, Seppelt, Rosemount, or Penfolds.

BROILED PEPPER-MARINATED FISH
WITH AVOCADO SALSA

My good friend Liz Wheeler, with whom I have sailed many nautical miles and written a yachting cookbook, can prepare marvelous meals in a 6-foot chop. Her spicy marinade works well with firm-fleshed fish (such as tuna, swordfish, red snapper, or shark), and beautifully complements the creamy-crunchy texture of the avocado salsa.

> 2 pounds fish fillets or steaks (at least 1-inch thick)
>   Salt
> 1 tablespoon West Indian Pepper Sauce (page 22) or a bottled
>   Caribbean-style sauce such as Isla Vieques Caribe Fire
> 2 medium garlic cloves, finely chopped
> 2 tablespoons chopped fresh cilantro
> ½ teaspoon ground cumin
> 3 tablespoons fresh lime or lemon juice
> 3 tablespoons fresh orange juice
> 4 tablespoons vegetable oil
>   Avocado Salsa (recipe follows)

Sprinkle the fish with salt and place in a single layer in a flat noncorrosive dish. Combine the remaining ingredients in a bowl and mix well. Pour the marinade over the fish. Cover and refrigerate for 1 to 2 hours.

When ready to cook, preheat broiler to high. Remove fish from marinade. Place on a foil-lined broiler pan. Broil 4 to 5 inches from heat for 8 to 10 minutes, until milky juices bead on the surface of the fish. Serve immediately with the avocado salsa on the side.

Serves 4.

AVOCADO SALSA

1 large, firm yet ripe avocado
⅓ lightly packed cup thinly sliced red onion
1 tablespoon fresh lime or lemon juice
1 tablespoon West Indian Pepper Sauce (page 22) or a bottled
   Caribbean-style sauce such as Isla Vieques Caribe Fire
Salt
1 tablespoon chopped, fresh cilantro

Cut the avocado lengthwise into quarters. Peel the quarters, then cut crosswise into ¼-inch slices. Toss the avocado lightly with the onion slices. Sprinkle with lime or lemon juice, hot sauce, salt, and cilantro and toss gently to combine.

Serves 4.

Variation: Add sliced, fresh papaya or orange segments with the membranes removed.

GRILLED SWORDFISH AND MIRLETON WITH MANGO SCOTCH BONNET BARBECUE SAUCE

In North Miami, chef Mark Militello of Mark's Place is putting himself on the culinary map with his deft weaving of tropical fruits, exotic root vegetables, and fresh fish. Favoring a light, California cooking style, he has created a dish with a remarkable range of flavors and textures—from the crisp mirleton (a tropical, pear-shaped squash) to the creamy avocado butter and rich swordfish grilled with a delectable mango Scotch bonnet sauce.

4 8-ounce fresh swordfish steaks
   Olive oil for brushing
   Salt and freshly ground black pepper to taste

AVOCADO BUTTER

2 ripe avocados
½ lime
¼ cup extra-virgin olive oil
   Salt and freshly ground black pepper to taste

GRILLED MIRLETON

2 mirletons
   Olive oil for brushing
2 cups Mango Scotch Bonnet Barbecue Sauce (page 23)

Brush the swordfish with oil and sprinkle with salt and pepper.

To prepare the avocado butter, puree the avocado flesh in a food processor with lime juice, working in the oil, salt, and pepper.

To grill the mirleton, cut lengthwise into ¼-inch slices. Brush the slices with oil and grill over medium heat until tender. Set aside and reserve. Grill the swordfish over a medium hardwood fire, continually basting with the Mango Scotch Bonnet Sauce. During the last minute of cooking the fish, place the mirleton back on the grill to warm.

To serve, arrange the mirleton in circles on dinner plates, placing swordfish in the center. Garnish each piece of fish with a tablespoon of avocado butter and serve immediately.

Serves 4.

SUGGESTED WINE: An Entre-Deux-Mers such as Chateau de Mirambeau or Alsatian Pinot Blanc. Two "sleepers" are Mirassou's White Burgundy (Pinot Blanc) and a fine Trebbiano from Ivan Tamas, if you can find one.

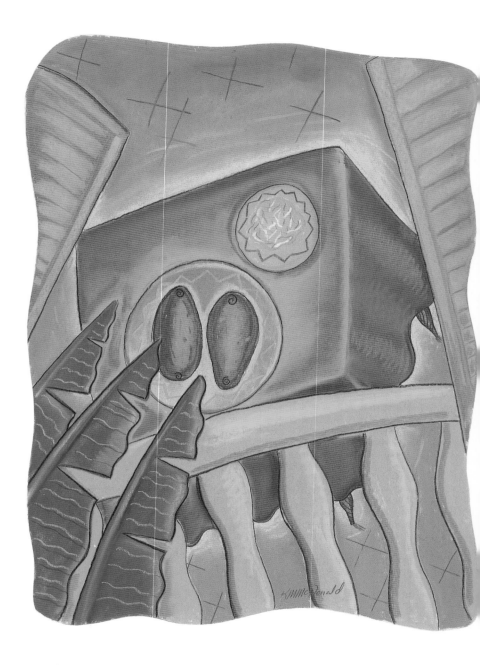

Side Dishes and Salads

Caribbean-Style Yams and Sweet Potatoes

This elegant dish can tolerate a spicy hot sauce, because the starch of the vegetables will absorb much of the heat. Even guests who are not hot-food lovers will love the flavors that the cinnamon and coriander in the hot sauce bring to the sweet potatoes, and the heat is present just enough to cast a subtle spotlight on the dish. This recipe also works well with just yams or sweet potatoes, although you won't get the interesting color combination without the two.

2 medium-sized, well-shaped yams
2 medium-sized, well-shaped sweet potatoes
3 tablespoons butter
2 tablespoons finely chopped scallions
2 teaspoons Spicy Island Hot Sauce (page 20) or a bottled Caribbean-style sauce such as Rebel Fire No. 3
Salt and freshly ground black pepper to taste

Preheat oven to 375 degrees. Scrub and dry the yams and sweet potatoes, and poke the skin of each once with a fork. Bake for about 45 minutes, or until tender.

Slit yams and sweet potatoes lengthwise and scrape out the pulp, taking care not to tear the skins. Reserve skins. In a bowl, combine the pulp with the butter, scallons, hot sauce, salt, and pepper, and mash with a fork. Taste and adjust seasonings. Turn on broiler. Stuff the mixture carefully into the potato skins and place on baking sheet. Place under broiler for 7 to 8 minutes, or until potatoes are hot and slightly browned on top.

Serves 4.

TOMATOES PROVENÇAL

Stuffed with garlic and other spices, this nicely seasoned side dish goes well with grilled lamb—but I also love it with veal or baked fish, which can cook in the same hot oven. While I used Adzhika, you could easily substitute Harissa, Smoky Salsa Picante, Pebre, or a Louisiana hot sauce. Just taste the stuffing before filling the tomatoes to check that the heat level matches your expectations.

> 2 *firm tomatoes*
> 1 *tablespoon chopped parsley*
> 3 *large garlic cloves, minced*
> ¾ *cup breadcrumbs*
> 1 *tablespoon scallions*
> 4 *teaspoons Adzhika (page 43) or a bottled Louisiana-style sauce such*
>   *as Bat's Brew*
>   *Salt and freshly ground pepper to taste*

Preheat oven to 350 degrees. Cut tomatoes in half and scoop out the pulp. Chop the pulp coarsely and put into a medium-sized bowl. Combine with remaining ingredients and mix well. Place the tomato hollows, cut side up, in a lightly buttered baking dish. Spoon tomato mixture gently into the hollows, forming slight mounds. Bake until crumbs appear golden, about 25 minutes. If desired, turn on broiler and put tomatoes under broiler for 5 minutes to brown further. Serve immediately.

Serves 4.

BAKED ACORN SQUASH

The sweet heat of maple syrup combined with hot sauce really comes through in the liquid pool that nestles in these baked self-contained shells.

- 2 acorn squash
- 2 tablespoons butter
- 2 tablespoons pure maple syrup
- 4 teaspoons Pineapple Curry Heat Wave (page 26) or a bottled Caribbean-style sauce such as Grand Anse Moko Jumbie
- 4 teaspoons chopped walnuts

Preheat oven to 350 degrees. Cut each squash in half. Scoop out the flesh and seeds and place squash, cut side up, in a shallow baking dish. Put into the hollow of each squash a pat of butter, ½ tablespoon syrup, and 1 teaspoon hot sauce. Mix gently and sprinkle with walnuts. Bake for 1 hour, or until flesh is soft.

Serves 4.

SHIITAKE RISOTTO SCOTCH BONNET

Thirty minutes spent tending this favorite Italian rice will be rewarded with a rich, creamy dish that can serve as a main course with a fresh green salad, or as a side dish to lamb or beef tenderloin. The goal is to seek a balance between the deep, woody flavors of the shiitakes and the delicate texture of the arborio rice, and to fleck it lightly with heat but not overwhelm the subtle flavors and saffron aroma of this dish. (Note: Do not substitute regular long-grain rice for the arborio.)

8–12 *medium to large Delftree shiitake mushrooms, stemmed*
  5 *tablespoons butter*
  2 *tablespoons shallots, minced*
  2 *cups arborio rice*
  2 *medium cloves garlic, minced*
  1 *tablespoon Death Wish (page 47) or a bottled specialty sauce such as Capital Punishment*
  1 *cup vermouth*
  5 *cups chicken broth*
    Pinch of saffron threads
    Romano cheese, freshly grated

Slice the mushroom caps into ¼-inch strips, halfing any strips longer than 2 inches. In a deep skillet, sauté over low heat the shiitake slices in melted butter for 3 minutes, or until the shiitakes give off their water. Add the shallots and cook for 2 minutes. Add the garlic and cook for 1 minute. Add the rice and swirl to coat with the butter. Add the hot sauce, vermouth, and 2 cups of the chicken broth.

Simmer over low heat, covered, adding additional chicken broth in ½-cup increments as the liquid is absorbed, stirring regularly. After 15 minutes, add the saffron, taste, and add more hot sauce if desired. Continue adding broth in increments, stirring, for an additional 15 minutes, or until the rice is cooked. (When done, the rice should have absorbed between 4 and 5 cups of the broth, and will be tender and loosely bound by the liquids.)

Serve immediately with grated Romano cheese.

Serves 6.

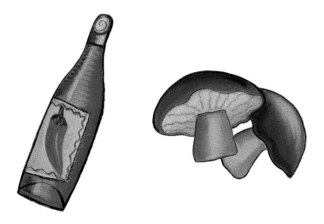

Push Around

While I was shopping at a small store in New Mexico, a Native American woman came in to buy dried chiles to make "push around." When I inquired about the recipe, she explained that she fried potatoes, onions, and garlic, then pushed it around in the frying pan with chiles until it was done. Made with hot sauce instead of chiles, "push around" is equally delicious. But a word of caution: don't add the hot sauce until just before removing potatoes from the stove. Frying the sauce will release clouds of capsaicin into the air, which will have you coughing and wheezing for hours—and understanding why South American Indians in the 1500s burned chiles as a smoke defense against the Spaniards.

QUICK LICKS

You can dress up many dishes with a few easy shakes. Some favorites:

SANDWICHES:

* Sun-dried tomatoes, fresh mozzarella, fresh basil, olive oil, and Smoky Salsa Picante (page 32) on a baguette.
* Fresh roasted green chiles sprinkled with Chipotle Red Sauce (page 34) and rolled into fresh tortillas.
* Mayonnaise mixed with hot sauce, folded into tuna fish with celery and onions, and served on toasted sourdough bread.

VEGETABLES:

* Whole vegetables (red bell peppers, zucchini, scallions, etc.) brushed with olive oil and hot sauce, then grilled.
* Chopped scallions, grated cheese, and hot sauce nestled into the crevice of a steaming baked potato.
* Lemon juice, butter, and a mild border sauce drizzled over steamed asparagus.

HORS D'OEUVRES:

* A little butter and black caviar spread on a thin cracker, squirted with fresh lemon juice and a drop of Cholula.

SERVING SECRETS:

* Hot sauce and eggs are terrific together, whether scrambled, folded into an omelet, or simply hardboiled.
* Hot sauce added to melted butter will spice up popcorn.
* The high vinegar content of Louisiana hot sauces makes them ideal accents for seafood.

SOUTH COAST HOMINY

Created by soaking shucked and hulled corn in vats filled with ash or lye, its starchiness texture and appealing bite make it a natural partner for hot sauce. Although this is a gulf-coast recipe, until a few decades ago hominy was also popular in New England. There you could find a "hominy man" traveling through villages, selling the enlarged corn that had been introduced to colonists by native Americans.

   2 *(15-ounce) cans hominy (1 white and 1 yellow), rinsed and drained*
   3 *tablespoons butter*
   1 *small onion, chopped*
   ½ *green bell pepper, chopped*
   3 *tablespoons flour*
   ½ *teaspoon dry mustard*
  1½ *cup milk*
   ½ *cup grated, sharp chedder cheese*
   ½ *cup chopped black olives*
   1 *roasted red pepper, chopped*
   2 *tablespoons F-16 (page 27) or a bottled Caribbean-style sauce such as West Indies Creole*
  1½ *cups buttered breadcrumbs to cover*
      Freshly ground black pepper

Place hominy in the bottom of a greased 9- x 13-inch casserole. Preheat oven to 375 degrees.

Sauté onion and bell pepper in butter until the onion becomes transparent. Sprinkle the flour and mustard over the onion and bell pepper, cooking about 1 minute over medium heat. Gradually add milk, continuing to cook until mixture begins to thicken. Add the cheese and continue cooking until it melts, then add olives, roasted red pepper, and hot sauce. Pour over the hominy, and top with buttered breadcrumbs and a few turns of black pepper. Bake for 30 minutes.

Serves 4 to 6.

HOT SAUCE LABEL DESIGN AWARDS

Given my love of hot sauce labels, I asked a few museum-world friends to judge the designs. And the winners are . . .

- Tabasco—When Edmund McIlhenny tipped the square label on its corner, he created a classic.
- Coyote Cocina—High Santa Fe style.
- Inner Beauty—The label's back-side is best, featuring lightning bolts, a dubious map, and good text.
- Capital Punishment—Chilehead meets *Mad Magazine*.
- Craig's—The contrast of the design subtlety in the color-coded chile border with the tonsil-revealing scream that it frames is marvelous.

HONORABLE MENTIONS

- Hot Sauce From Hell—for the dripping wax seal, which looks like the devil's doing.
- Sunny Caribee—for the little sombrero lid.
- Cholula—handsome design with a great wooden cap.
- Baumer's A.B.—almost generic in its simplicity, but is there any doubt about its authenticity?
- Pickapeppa—elegant in the old Caribbean style, with shimmering bronze ink.
- Spitfire—A good melding of British signage and Caribbean heat.
- Busha Browne's Pukka Sauce—Crown Colony design made contemporary.

OKIE OKRA SALAD

Introduced to the Americas by African slaves, okra was a typical ingredient in Caribbean cooking by the 1600s and today is used extensively throughout the South. Oklahoma food often has a Southern hand, and I thank my mother-in-law for introducing this Yankee to okra and this delicious salad. The crispiness of the fried okra contrasts wonderfully with the juicy tomatoes, both of which come alive with the hot sauce.

   1 *pound fresh okra, stems removed, cut into ½-inch rounds*
   1 *egg, slightly beaten*
  ½ *cup flour*
  ½ *cup corn meal*
  ½ *teaspoon baking powder*
   1 *teaspoon salt*
    Freshly ground black pepper
    Vegetable oil for frying
   2 *juicy ripe tomatoes, chopped*
   4 *green onions, chopped*
1–2 *tablespoons Louisiana Red (page 18) or a bottled Louisiana-style sauce such as Arizona Gunslinger*

Combine okra and egg in a bowl. In another bowl, combine flour, corn meal, baking powder, salt, and pepper. Add only enough of the flour mixture to the okra to coat. Heat oil in skillet and add the dusted okra, frying until golden and crisp, about 20 minutes.

While okra is cooking, combine tomatoes, onions, and hot sauce in a salad bowl. When okra is done, drain on paper towels, then toss with tomato mixture. (If you're not serving immediately, keep the okra separate until the last moment to retain the crispiness.) Serve hot or at room temperature.

Serves 4.

SOUL-SLAW

One of my best college experiences was singing in an all-black gospel choir. I wasn't particularly religious—nor was I black—but the music got into my bones, and when the director suggested I audition, I jumped at the chance. On Sundays we'd take road trips to small A.M.E. churches in Ohio and Indiana. We'd sing at services that lasted 3 or 4 hours, after which the church ladies would lay on unbelievable spreads in the basement—fried chicken, corn bread, collard greens, and coleslaw. When I inquired whether this beautiful cabbage dish was even remotely related to what I'd seen in delis, one woman laughed and said, "Girl, this is *soul*-slaw."

That was a few years ago, but the good memories linger, and this coleslaw is in honor of those A.M.E. ladies. The heat in this dish is subtle and surprising, coming late at the back of your mouth.

    1 *cup mayonnaise*
    ¼ *cup white vinegar*
    1 *tablespoon sugar*
    1½ *teaspoon Dijon mustard*
    3–4 *tablespoons Louisiana Red (page 18) or a bottled Louisiana-style*
          sauce such as Dos Gringos or Hot Lava
          Freshly ground black pepper
    ½ *head green cabbage, shredded*
    ½ *head red cabbage, shredded*
    2 *carrots, grated*

In a small bowl, whisk together the mayonnaise, vinegar, sugar, mustard, hot sauce, and black pepper. Taste and correct seasoning. In a large bowl, toss the cabbages and carrots. Pour on half of the dressing slowly, mixing into the salad. Add additional dressing until salad becomes glossy. Cover and refrigerate for several hours.

Makes 4 cups.

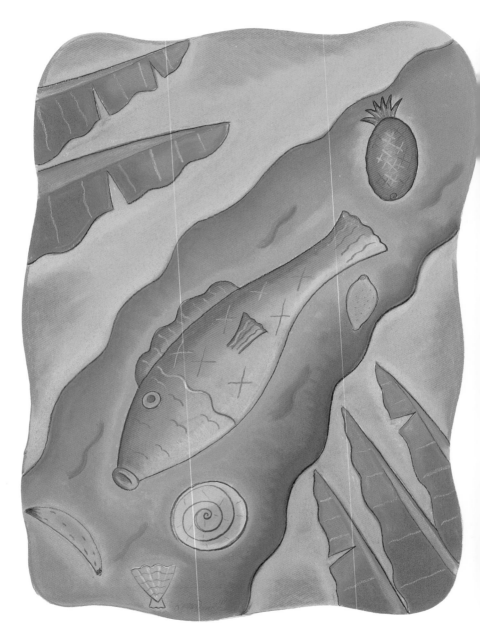

INNER BEAUTY TROPICAL FRUIT RELISH

This relish is terrific with grilled chicken or fish, and very popular at the East Coast Grill in Boston. The hot-fruit combination is used in many cultures, particularly in India and Africa. You might want to start slow with the hot sauce and increase it to taste, depending on your guests' attitude.

>   1 ripe mango, banana, papaya, and pineapple, all cut into ½-inch cubes
>   Juice of two limes
>   1 small red onion, finely chopped
>   10 cilantro leaves, chopped
>   1–3 tablespoons Inner Beauty Real Hot Sauce or Pineapple Curry Heat Wave (page 26)

In a large bowl, combine the fruit with lime juice, onion, and cilantro. Add the hot sauce, 1 tablespoon at a time to achieve desired heat level. Allow the flavors to blend for an hour, then spoon onto grilled chicken or fish.

Makes approximately 2½ cups.

Heaven on Seventh

If you're in Chicago, don't miss Heaven on Seventh, a coffee shop that serves some of the best Cajun food outside of Louisiana and has a hot sauce collection nearing 300 bottles. Drop by with two hot sauces chef Jimmy Bannos hasn't seen, and he'll treat you to a bowl of gumbo with corn bread on the side.

SAVORY VINAIGRETTE

I love green salads made with several kinds of lettuce, fresh basil, parsley, watercress, and serve them after the main course to cleanse the palate and make way for dessert. This vinaigrette has a subtle lift, with more spice than heat.

1 teaspoon Dijon Double Hot (page 48) or even a bottled Caribbean-style sauce such as Spitfire
⅛ cup Pique (page 14)
⅛ cup balsamic vinegar
½ teaspoon salt
⅛ teaspoon freshly ground black pepper
¾ cup extra-virgin olive oil
1 large garlic clove, minced
1 tablespoon finely chopped scallion

Combine ingredients in a jar and shake well.

Makes 1 cup.

PIQUANT TOMATO SALAD

Show off your fresh garden tomatoes by tossing them with this silky dressing that brings out their ripe sweetness. I often serve this salad with a simple grilled fish dinner, accompanied by corn on the cob and bread.

16 tiny whole, red tomatoes, halved
16 tiny whole, yellow tomatoes, halved
½ cup loosely shredded baby lettuce or frisée
12 fresh basil leaves, shredded

DRESSING

1 tablespoon balsamic vinegar
2 garlic cloves, minced
2 teaspoons Dijon Double Hot (page 48)
   Juice of ½ lemon
   Salt and freshly ground pepper to taste
2 teaspoons finely chopped shallots or chives
3 tablespoons extra-virgin olive oil

Combine salad ingredients in a medium-size bowl and toss well. In a small jar, combine dressing ingredients and shake well. Pour over salad and serve immediately.

Serves 4.

"When I cook, I never measure or weigh anything. I cook by vibration. I can tell by the look and smell of it . . . Different strokes for different folks. Do your thing your way."
   —Vertamae Smart-Grosvenor

"Hot Potato" Potato Salad

In this delicious salad from Connecticut writer Mary Goodbody, you'll find that the heat intensifies as the salad marinates. (For less intensity, omit the jalapeño.)

> 2 *pounds small new potatoes (cut into 1-inch pieces if too big)*
> 1 *jalapeño pepper, chopped*
> 1 *½-inch fresh ginger root, peeled and finely chopped*
> 1 *large clove garlic, crushed*
>   *Juice of 3 limes*
> 1 *tablespoon cider vinegar*
> 3 *tablespoons West Indian Pepper Sauce (page 22) or a bottled*
>   *Caribbean-style sauce such as Papaya Pepper Tropic Hot Sauce*
> 1 *tablespoon light soy sauce*
> 1 *tablespoon honey*
> 6 *tablespoons vegetable oil*
> 2 *teaspoons salt*
>   *Freshly ground black pepper to taste*
> ½ *medium-sized red onion, thinly sliced*
> 4 *ounces Monterey Jack cheese, cubed (optional)*
> 3 *tablespoons chopped cilantro or parsley*
>   *Arugula, for serving*

Drop the potatoes in a large pot of boiling water. Cook, uncovered, over medium-high heat for 20 to 25 minutes until the potatoes are fork-tender.

Meanwhile, combine the jalapeño, ginger, garlic, lime juice, vinegar, hot sauce, soy sauce, and honey. Slowly add the oil, whisking constantly. Season with salt and pepper.

Drain the cooked potatoes and transfer them to a large bowl. Toss the warm potatoes with the dressing. Set aside for 20 to 30 minutes to cool to lukewarm.

Toss the salad with the sliced onion, cheese, and cilantro. Chill for at least 1 hour. Serve chilled on a bed of arugula.

Serves 8.

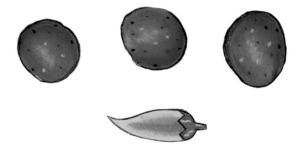

A GUIDE TO CHILES

While people differ in their reaction to the same chile's heat, a broad heat range has been calculated based on a standard developed in 1912 by pharmacologist Wilbur Scoville, who calculated the amount of water required to neutralize capsaicin's pungency. Capsaicin levels are now determined by computerized machinery, but the Scoville standard still holds, with bell peppers scoring 0 Scoville units, jalapeños rating 2500 to 5000 units, and habañeros rating a scorching 150,000 to 300,000 units. Based on this standard, chiles are rated 1 through 10, with 10 the hottest. Be cautioned, however, that chiles can vary in heat from crop to crop, and even bush to bush. You have to taste to be sure!

AJI.

With a fruity flavor, this orange-red scorcher is often used in sauces, and can be substituted for habañeros. (In Spanish, aji is also generic for peppers.) (7–8)

ANAHEIM.

Commonly called a long green or red chile, and virtually indistinguishable from the New Mexico green or red from which it stems (with the exception perhaps of having a slightly smoother, waxier skin). In general, if the chile is milder (2–3 on the heat scale), it tends to be classified as an Anaheim, which are delicious roasted, stuffed, used in hot sauces, or ground into chile powder. The reds are slightly sweeter and often used in ristras. (2–3)

ANCHO.

A dried poblano, with varieties called mulato (light brown) or negro (black), anchos ("wide" in Spanish) are used extensively in Mexican moles and cooked sauces. With aromas of chocolate and tobacco, this aromatic chile has strong berry accents. Adding a marvelous, deep red color to hot sauces, it nicely balances the searing heat of other chiles. The seeds can be hot. (4)

BANANA PEPPER.

Also known as güero, Sante Fe Grande, or Hungarian wax, and similar to its thin-skinned cousin, the chawa. Pale yellow to pale green, ripening to orange and red, this long tapered fruit has heat varying from 0 for the sweet banana pepper to 6 or more for the Hungarian wax. It is often pickled, stuffed, or used in sauces. (0–6)

BIRD PEPPER.

See chiltecpin.

CASCABEL.

Sometimes used fresh, more often the Mexican cascabel ("jingle bell") is dried into a reddish-brown sphere the size of a walnut, whose paper-thin walls and jingling seeds lend it its name. Used in sauces and salsas, the cascabel has a smoky, tannic bite. (4–5)

CAYENNE.

Lipstick red, the cayenne is a cousin of the tabasco pepper, and is also known as the de Arbol ("from the tree") or ginnie pepper. It is primarily used fresh in Louisiana hot sauces or ground into cayenne pepper. (8–9)

CHERRY.

Orange to deep red and resembling a cherry (also known as a Hungarian cherry), this usually mild pepper is often pickled or added to sauces for its sweetness and fleshiness. (1–5)

CHILTEPE.

With an orange-red body and a pronounced bend, the dried tepin resembles a cayenne, with a similar up-front heat, though less ferocious. (6)

CHILTECPIN.

Also called chiltepin, tepin, bird pepper, and chile bravo ("wild chile"), this tiny, ovoid-shaped pepper packs a tremendous, front-of-the-mouth heat. Related to the the pequin, the chiltecpin is orange or red and used both dried and fresh to season beans, stews, and many cooked dishes. While the heat fades fast, it gives hot sauces a quick hit that announces you mean business. (8–9)

CHIPOTLE.

These are jalapeños that have been smoked and transmogrified into dark brown, gnarled and skeletal dried chiles. Uniquely Mexican, chipotles are redolent of burning pecan and fruit woods, and add the fifth dimension to sauces. (5)

DUTCH.

Vivid red, with beautiful skin, this fruity chile from Holland makes a flavorful substitute for the smaller, red Thai chile, and is frequently found in supermarkets. (6)

FRESNO.

Succulent and sweet, fresnos ripen to a bright red and resemble jalapeños, though are sometimes hotter. Used green for pickling, sauces, and seasonings, when mature red they are delicious roasted and used in sauces. Picklers also prize a smaller yellow version known as the cascabella, whose name ("beautiful skin") reveals its additional usage as an ornamental. (6–7)

HABAÑERO.
With its many varieties and names—congo pepper (Trinidad), Bahama Mama (Bahamas), datil pepper (Florida)—the habañero's pleated, lantern shape is unique, as is its incendiary fire, which is smooth and quick-lived. Ranging from green to yellow, orange, and red, fresh habañeros have a distinctly fruity aroma, which goes well with sauces, seafood, and tropical fruits. (10)

JALAPEÑO.
Although sometimes considered the sine-qua-non of heat, on the Scoville scale jalapeños fall in the respectable middle ground. Ranging from a thick-fleshed green to bright red when ripe, jalapeños are perhaps the most famous chile, with their image today adorning everything from pot holders to boxer shorts. Their excellent flavor/heat combination adds zest to many dishes and sauces. (5–6)

KOREAN.
Green Korean chiles are often found in Southeast Asian markets and go from sweet to hot as they age. With a distinctive grassy taste, they are often used in Korean relishes and marinades. (6–7)

LONG GREEN.
See Anaheim.

MACHO.
Related to the pequin, this small fresh chile is as hot as it sounds, pushing the habañero for fire power, but not flavor. (9–10)

MIRASOL.

The woody, slightly acidic taste of the mirasol ("looking at the sun") makes this a good, slightly scaled-down substitute for New Mexico reds. Dried, it's known as guajillo (and sometimes cascabel, because the seeds rattle when dried, although these should not be confused with the round variety discussed above), with a medium heat and earthy flavor that enriches sauces and other dishes. (3–5)

MORA.

Like the chipotle, the dried mora is a smoked jalapeño, though the mora (and its sisters morita and mora grande) retains a deep, red color, providing mesquite flavors. (6)

NEW MEXICO RED AND GREEN.

Probably brought from Mexico to New Mexico in the late 1500s, New Mexico chiles have a wide range of culinary uses, both fresh and dried, from sauces to tamales. They are also known as Anaheim chiles, although as California chile production is overtaken by New Mexico, common usage is gradually replacing the name Anaheim with New Mexicos. For kitchen stock, it's hard to beat a ristra of dried New Mexico reds. (2–5)

PASILLA.

Also called chile negro, this long, dark brown dried chile is mild and mellow, and essential for mole sauces. (3–5)

PEQUIN.

Lozenge-shaped and bright red, pequins are used dried or fresh, and after the initial flame-up they leave a delightful citric aftertaste. Known in Peru as "pipi de mono" (monkey's little dick), they are so popular in Texas that people carry them in pill boxes for quick heat.

Combined with mellower chiles, pequins make an excellent, Roman candle-like hot sauce. (8–9)

PETER PEPPER.

Mainly an ornamental, but, oh, what an ornament it makes! (This pepper takes on a rather realistic anatomical shape as it grows.) A smaller variety is called little boy. (7–8)

PIMENTO.

This large, sweetheart-shaped chile is similar in taste to red bell peppers, but with enough zing to make it interesting. Used fresh as a garnish, or dried and ground as paprika. (1)

POBLANO.

Somewhat mild, ranging in color from dark green to brick red. The red variety is slightly sweeter, and when dried it is known as an ancho. Roasted, it adds a smoky flavor to sauces. (3)

ROCOTILLO.

Although related to the habañero, the carmine red rocotillo has only a fraction of the heat. Its fresh fruit is crisp and sweet and is sometimes confused with its hotter relative, the rocoto. Some chile connoiseurs consider this to be the finest "eating" chile in the world. (7–8)

ROCOTO.

Sometimes called manzana, this rare pepper with black seeds ranges from evergreen to yellow-orange to deep red. It is used fresh in sauces and salsas, with its heat said to rival or surpass the habañero, which perhaps explains why Peruvians call it gringo huanuchi—"gringo killer." (8–9)

SCOTCH BONNET.

This slightly smaller, Jamaican version of the habañero takes its name from its resemblance to a floppy Scotsman's bonnet. The colors have brighter hues than the habañero, but the intense heat and tropical fruitiness are the same. (10)

SERRANO.

Bright green or red, these bullet-shaped pods have a sharp, lasting heat that is useful in accenting hot sauces and won't get lost in rich sauces. They are not extremely flavorful on their own, however. (7–8)

TABASCO.

Used almost exclusively in the McIlhenny sauce of the same name. The thin-skinned tabasco has a slight vegetable flavor, along with its well-known heat. (9)

THAI.

Turning from green to bright red, Thai chiles are rich with oils that coat the mouth with lasting heat. A good substitute for serranos, with 1 Thai equaling 3 serranos. (7–8)

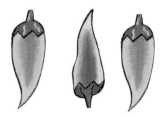

MAIL-ORDER SOURCES

If you have trouble finding hot sauces, chiles, or other items, you can mail-order from the following sources:

HOT SAUCES

Coyote Cocina, 1364 Rufina Circle #1, Santa Fe, NM 87501
800.866.HOWL
200 hot sauces, 17 dried chiles and Southwestern items.

Flamingo Flats, Box 441, St. Michael's, MD 21663
800.468.8841
300 hot sauces and 35 Jamaican Jerk sauces. Mail-order is year-round; the shop is open Easter to Christmas.

Lotta Hotta, 7895 Mastin, Overland Park, KS 66204
800.LOTTHOT
Many sauces (including their own fiery brand), books, aprons, etc.

Mo Hotta Mo Betta, Box 4136, San Luis Obispo, CA 93403
800.462.3220
Hundreds of hot sauces, dried chiles, and gifts of fire.

Peppers Gift Shop, 2009 Highway 1, Dewey Beach, DE 19971
800.998.FIRE
Over 200 hot sauces, located next to the Starboard Restaurant that features 300 hot sauces for sampling on weekends.

Sambet's Cajun Store, 8644 Spicewood Springs Road, Suite F, Austin, TX 78759
800.472.6238
265 hot sauces, as well as Cajun books and foods.

Chile Hill Emporium, Box 9100, Bernalillo, NM 87004
505.867.3294
New Mexican products including unsprayed ristras, pure chili powders, and many Southwestern books.

Chile Pepper Emporium, 328 San Felipe N.W., Albuquerque, NM 87104
505.242.7538
Cookbooks, chile-related gift items, unusual seasoning packets, and chile powders.

Colorado Spice Company, 5030 Nome Street, Unit A, Denver, CO 80239
800.67SPICE
Hot sauces; over 15 ground, flaked and whole dried chiles; and exotic herbs and spices.

D. L. Jardine's, Jardine Ranch, Buda, TX 78610
800.544.1880
On a ranch in "Buda-ful" Texas, Blazin' Saddle and Texas Champagne hot sauces, and other Texas specialties.

Don Alfonso, Box 201988, Austin, TX 78720-1988
800.456.6100
Roasted fresh New Mexican chiles, 24 dried chiles, 13 chile powders, 10 types of seeds, and Don Alfonso's own sauces.

Frieda's, Inc., Box 58488, Los Angeles, CA 90058
800.241.1771
9 fresh chiles, 7 dried chiles, as well as tropical fruits.

Hot Heads, Inc., 3307 Kissel Hill Road, Lititz, PA 17543
800.531.2407
For true chileheads, Hot Heads offers Capital Punishment and Last Rites, 15 dried peppers, and weird T-shirts.

Isla Vieques Condiment Company, Box 1496, Vieques, Puerto Rico 00765
809.741.0848
High-quality sauces made in Vieques.

Island Bound, Box 1268, St. Thomas, US Virgin Islands 00804
800.424.8055
Over 25 Caribbean hot sauces.

Sunny Caribbee Spice Co., Box 3237 VDA, St. Thomas, US Virgin Islands 00803
809.494.2178
Makers of Caribbean sauces and spices, handsomely packaged.

Stonewall Chili Pepper Company, Box 241, Highway 290 East, Stonewall, TX 78671-9998
800.232.2995
5 kinds of seeds, dried chiles and powders, 12 fresh chiles in season, and Stonewall's own food products.

Tabasco Country Store, McIlhenny Company, Avery Island, LA 70513
800.634.9599
Tabasco and McIlhenny Farms food products and Cajun specialties.

The Pepper Gal, Box 23006, Ft. Lauderdale, FL 33307-3006
305.537.5540

Ground zero for pepper seeds, offering some 120 hot varieties, 36 ornamentals, and 60 sweets.

Delftree Farm, Box 460, Pownal, VT 05261
800.243.3742

Organic shiitakes shipped within 48 hours of being picked.

Hot Licks Poster, c/o JT[2] Productions, 560 North Hoosac Road, Williamstown, MA 01267
413.458.2882

Where can you find Inner Beauty, Capital Punishment, and Hellfire & Damnation? In a colorful Hot Licks poster that celebrates 100 of my favorite hot sauces. To order, send $14 to the address above, or phone for information. Enjoy those hot licks!

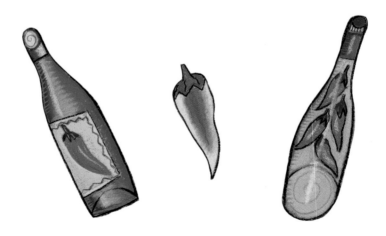

In researching this book, I discovered many terrific places serving spicy food. Some were noted culinary shrines, but others were not so obvious—roadside bars, cafes, and obscure hole-in-the-walls that were simply serving good food and hot licks. Who would ever think, after all, that a bar on a snowmobile trail in the Adirondacks would dish up chicken wings marinated in an incendiary sauce called Armageddon (and reward those who survive it)? I enjoyed this "research" so much that I dubbed it my trail of flame, and got so many requests that I'm putting together a simple restaurant guide. If you know of a restaurant that belongs on the Trail, drop me a line at JT² Productions, 560 North Hoosac Road, Williamstown, MA 01267. I'd love to hear from you.

BIBLIOGRAPHY

Andrews, Jean. *Peppers: The Domesticated Capsicums.* Austin: University of Texas Press, 1984.

Christian Woman's Exchange of New Orleans. *The Creole Cookery Book.* New Orleans: T. H. Thomason, 1885.

DeWitt, Dave, and Nancy Gerlach. *The Whole Chile Pepper Book.* Boston: Little, Brown and Company, 1990.

Grimes, William. *Straight Up or On the Rocks.* New York: Simon & Schuster, 1993.

Hemingway, Ernest. *Islands in the Stream.* New York: Charles Scribner's Sons, 1970.

Lang, Jenifer Harvey, ed. *Larousse Gastronomique.* New York: Crown Publishers, 1988.

Lang, Jenifer Harvey. *Tastings.* New York: Crown Publishers, 1986.

McIlhenny, Paul, with Barbara Hunter. *The Tabasco Cookbook.* New York: Clarkson Potter, 1993.

Miller, Mark. *Coyote Cafe.* Berkeley: Ten Speed Press, 1989.

Miller, Mark. *The Great Chile Book.* Berkeley: Ten Speed Press, 1991.

Naj, Amal. *Peppers: A Story of Hot Pursuits.* New York: Alfred A. Knopf, 1992.

Robbins, Jim. "It Feels Like Your Lips Are Going to Fall Off." *Smithsonian,* January 1992.

Schweid, Richard. *Hot Peppers.* Berkeley: Ten Speed Press, 1987.

Smart-Grosvenor, Vertamae. *Vibration Cooking.* New York: Ballantine Books, 1970.

Solomon, Jay. "In Search of the Scotch Bonnet." *Chile Pepper.* January/February 1993.

Walsh, Robb. "Pass the Salsa, Xnipec!" *Chile Pepper,* July/August 1991.

TABLE OF EQUIVALENTS

The exact equivalents in the following tables have been rounded for convenience.

US/UK	METRIC
oz = ounce	g = gram
lb = pound	kg = kilogram
in = inch	mm = millimeter
ft = foot	cm = centimeter
tbl = tablespoon	ml = milliliter
fl oz = fluid ounce	l = liter
qt = quart	

WEIGHTS

US/UK	Metric
1 oz	30 g
2 oz	60 g
3 oz	90 g
4 oz (¼ lb)	125 g
5 oz (⅓ lb)	155 g
6 oz	185 g
7 oz	220 g
8 oz (½ lb)	250 g
10 oz	315 g
12 oz (¾ lb)	375 g
14 oz	440 g
16 oz (1 lb)	500 g
1½ lb	750 g
2 lb	1 kg
3 lb	1.5 kg

OVEN TEMPERATURES

°F	°C	Gas
250	120	½
275	140	1
300	150	2
325	160	3
350	180	4
375	190	5
400	200	6
425	220	7
450	230	8
475	240	9
500	260	10

LIQUIDS

US	Metric	UK
2 tbl	30 ml	1 fl oz
¼ cup	60 ml	2 fl oz
⅓ cup	80 ml	3 fl oz
½ cup	125 ml	4 fl oz
⅔ cup	160 ml	5 fl oz
¾ cup	180 ml	6 fl oz
1 cup	250 ml	8 fl oz
1½ cups	375 ml	12 fl oz
2 cups	500 ml	16 fl oz
4 cups/1 qt	1 l	32 fl oz

HOT LICKS INDEX